The Book of Exodus

D1127934

The Book of Exodus

An Exposition by

Charles R. Erdman

BAKER BOOK HOUSE
Grand Rapids, Michigan 49506

Copyright 1949 by
Fleming H. Revell Company
Paperback edition issued 1982 by
Baker Book House
with permission of copyright owner

ISBN: 0-8010-3376-4

PHOTOLITHOPRINTED BY CUSHING - MALLOY, INC.
ANN ARBOR, MICHIGAN, UNITED STATES OF AMERICA

To

*The Greater Glory
of the Redeemer*

Introduction

THIS book records *the birth of a nation*. The name
"Exodus," meaning a "departure," an "outgoing," was
given properly by the Greek translators of the Old Testament, for the early part of the record describes the deliverance of Israel from bondage in Egypt. Yet the story
is much more than this. It relates the journey of the
people from Egypt to Sinai, the covenant made with
Jehovah on the basis of the divinely revealed Law, and
the erection of the Tabernacle as the place and symbol
of worship. Thus the book might be divided into two
parts, The Origin and Deliverance of the People (Chs.
1 to 18) and the Organization and Consecration of the
Nation (Chs. 19 to 40). However, it may be helpful to
fix the thought, in the first part, on both (1) the *Deliverance* and (2) the *Journey*, and, in the second part,
on (3) the *Law* and (4) the *Tabernacle*. These four
words form a fair summary of the story, which as a whole
may be described as a record of *The Redemption and
Consecration of Israel as the Covenant People of God*.

The central figure of the book is *Moses*, one of
the most colossal and majestic characters in the history
of the world. He was a great general; not only did he
liberate a race of slaves, but he guided and sustained
them for forty years in a desert; he organized them into
a free commonwealth, and he transformed them into a

formidable army, which under the leadership of Joshua conquered the land of Canaan.

He was a wise legislator. The legal code of every civilized nation is based upon the laws which he enacted. Whatever he may have borrowed or inherited from previous systems or practices, he infused all with a new spirit, and elevated all moral conduct by basing it on the relationship of man to a spiritual and holy God.

Moses possessed literary gifts of a high order. He was a gifted poet, an impressive orator, and a careful historian. He was a true statesman, trained in the court of Egypt, he created a nation which was to make for itself a place of abiding influence in the history of the world.

He was supremely "the man of God." His proverbial meekness, his undaunted courage, his heroic fidelity, were all expressions of his unquestioning faith. Men were taught by him to believe in a Divine Being who is active in nature and in history, who is "full of compassion and gracious, slow to anger and plenteous in mercy and truth."

With all propriety, Moses has been regarded as a type of Christ, a true prophet, a prevailing intercessor, the saviour of his people.

The Deliverance of Israel from bondage in Egypt (Chs. 1 to 15) has been seen as a symbol of the *redemption* of men from the dominion of sin and death. The supreme chapter of this section (Ch. 12) describes the *Passover,* an annual festival which was established as an abiding memorial of the deliverance secured by Moses, and which became a prophecy of the redemption to be wrought by Christ.

The experiences of the wilderness *Journey* (Chs. 15 to 18) have furnished the people of God with figures of speech which have described the *Providence* whereby believers receive guidance, protection, and support on their journey through "the wilderness of this world."

The *Law* (Chs. 19 to 24) contains the supreme expression of the will of God for the guidance of man. The great message of this section is *Obedience*, for it was on the ground of their promised observance of this law that the covenant was formed whereby Israel was to become a holy nation under the rule of Jehovah as King.

The erection of the *Tabernacle* gave to the people a visible symbol of the meaning of *Worship* (Chs. 25 to 40). It taught them the necessity for holiness, and the significance of sacrifice and mediation for those who sought access to God.

Thus Exodus is not only a book of history, but also is a handbook of religion. Its story of redemption and its directions for a redeemed people relate it vitally to the theme of the entire Bible, which may be stated as the *Revelation of redemption through Christ* in order to bring about the final establishment of the Kingdom of God on earth.

Contents

I

THE DELIVERANCE EXODUS 1:1 to 15:21

THE ORIGIN AND OPPRESSION OF THE PEOPLE. [Ch. 1.]

ISRAEL is the name given to the patriarch Jacob when he wrestled with the angel, before crossing the Jabbok, as he returned to Canaan from Mesopotamia. It came to be used of all his descendants, who were known collectively as "Israel," or as the "Sons of Jacob," or the "Children of Israel."

Thus, in narrating the origin of this race, the Book of Exodus opens with the names of the actual sons of Jacob (Ch. 1:1) and then employs the same term, "Children of Israel," when recording the growth of the people (vs. 6) and their oppression by Pharaoh (vss. 9, etc).

The names of the twelve sons of the patriarch, and the statement that they "came into Egypt," forms a close tie to the book of Genesis (Gen. 46:8–27). Indeed, the first word of Exodus, "now," which may be translated correctly as "and," is a link indicating that these first two books of the Bible are a connected narrative. To understand the story which follows, one needs to be reminded of the promises made to Abraham and Isaac and Jacob, and to review the romantic career of Joseph.

The character of this pure and princely Prime

Minister of Egypt contrasts strangely with that of his crude and cruel brothers, yet all were instruments of divine providence. Their experiences illustrate a true philosophy of history. Through them God was effecting His purpose of bringing into being a people from which was to come the Saviour of the world.

According to Genesis, his brothers sold Joseph as a slave into Egypt. As Exodus opens, their descendants are found in Egyptian bondage. Joseph was lifted from slavery and imprisonment to the place of supreme power; Exodus will relate the deliverance of Israel from bondage and its emergence as a nation consecrated to the service of God.

Joseph was brought into Egypt by the cruelty of his brothers; they were brought thither by his generosity and pardoning grace. This was effecting the divine plan. The sons of Jacob could never have developed into a powerful race in the land of Canaan. There they were surrounded by hostile tribes and in possession of no considerable portion of land. In Egypt they were given possession of Goshen, the spacious and most fertile portion of Egypt. There, during the four centuries which followed, they developed into a powerful and vigorous and formidable race.

It must not be supposed that the migration from Canaan to Egypt was composed of only the seventy souls named in the narrative. There were the sons of Jacob and their "households," but the latter included wives, children, grandchildren, and large numbers of servants and retainers. It was no insignificant band of emigrants, but a clan of large proportions and power. In the rich land of Goshen, under the patronage of Joseph, and enjoying the favor of successive kings, "The children of Israel," as we read, "were fruitful, and increased abundantly, and multiplied, and waxed exceeding mighty; and the land was filled with them."

It was this prosperity which invited disaster. "There arose up a new king over Egypt, which knew not Joseph." Indeed, centuries had passed since the death of the great statesman who had enjoyed the favor of Pharaoh and had saved the nation in a time of famine. The very name of Joseph may have been unknown to this "new king" who ascends the throne, who has no reason for feeling gratitude toward Israel, but who sees in so powerful an alien race a possible threat to his own sovereignty. He determines to weaken if not to destroy the rapidly increasing people. To secure the co-operation of the Egyptian rulers, or to justify his cruelty, he probably exaggerates the political peril which he discerns. "And he said unto his people, Behold, the people of the children of Israel are more and mightier than we: Come on, let us deal wisely with them; lest they multiply, and it come to pass, that, when there falleth out any war, they join also unto our enemies, and fight against us, and so get them up out of the land."

It is not at all probable that Israel planned a migration, or that they would have proved treacherous and joined invaders from the east. They were not a military but a pastoral people. For centuries they had dwelt peaceably and contentedly in their homes, caring for their flocks and herds amid the fertile fields of Goshen. However, the fear and hatred of the king were inflamed by jealousy. The "wise dealing" he planned and put into effect was forced labor, which developed into the most cruel form of slavery.

"They did set over them taskmasters to afflict them with their burdens." They were compelled to labor, not only in cultivating the fields, but in digging canals, building dikes, and constructing store cities and arsenals. During interminable hours, under the scorching sun, their bare bodies bleeding from the cruel lash, they were made "to serve with rigour," and their lives were "bitter with hard bondage."

"But the more they afflicted them, the more they multiplied and grew." This was the first appearance in history of anti-Semitism, and it furnished the pattern which has been repeated again and again in the tragic centuries which have followed. The Hebrew race ever has been hated. Some of the ill will has been deserved. However, usually the enmity has been fostered by suspicion and jealousy and fear. Severe persecutions and oppressions have been inflicted, but the race has survived them all. The vitality of the Israelites has been amazing. The preservation of the Jew has been a mystery and a miracle.

In the case of Pharaoh, when cruel oppression failed to check the growth of the enslaved people, he adopted a secret measure even more Satanic. He ordered the midwives, who assisted the Israelitish women at the time of childbirth, to put every male child to death. This order was defied. They gave the excuse that the Israelites did not need their services. This was only partially true; and God rewarded them, not for their deception, but for their courage in defying the king. He gave them households and families of their own.

However, Pharaoh was not to be foiled. He now gave openly a royal decree that every son born to Hebrew parents should be cast into the river Nile. The situation of Israel was desperate. The future was black with terror and tragedy. If the race was to survive, a deliverer and saviour must appear.

THE DELIVERER. [Chs. 2:1 to 7:7.]

The Birth and Rescue of Moses. (Ch. 2:1-10). The record of the birth of Moses is surprisingly simple and unadorned, but the story of his rescue when a babe reads like of romance of divine providence. In the case of a national hero the life story usually is begun with a wealth of details as to his ancestry and circumstances. For the founder of a great religion his origin usually is glorified by elaborate legends or fantastic myths. Here, however, we have only this word: "There went a man of the house of Levi, and took to wife a daughter of Levi." These parents of Moses are not even named. They commonly are believed to have been Amram and Jochebed. Such seems to be the specific statement of Scripture (Ex. 6:20; Nums. 26:59). If literally true, then Jochebed was not only the wife of Amram but also his aunt. However, as "a daughter of Levi" means a descendant of the son of Jacob who had died centuries before, so Amram and Jochebed may be ancestral titles. To the author of Exodus, however, these names seem to be of no significance. He had made it plain that these parents were obscure slaves and members of a hated race. Yet to them was born a son who was to be the saviour of a people from which was to come the Saviour of the world.

It was a time of tragedy and terror. The babe at his birth was under sentence of death. The deliverer needed to be delivered. His rescue involved a number of factors: a mother's love, the cry of an infant, the compassion of a princess, the shrewdness of a sister, and the faith of godly parents. The cry of the babe is worthy of mention. At least, it can illustrate the fact that seeming trifles may be essential links in a chain of events which brings to pass issues of vast importance. By way of contrast, the faith of the mother was not a trifling matter. It is true that it is not even mentioned by the historian. Yet the New Testament records it as the real explanation of what occurred, and in this record both father and mother are united in their undaunted courage. "By faith Moses when he was born, was hid three months by his parents, because they saw he was a goodly child; and they were not afraid of the king's commandment." This, then, was the story. A humble woman, a Hebrew slave, defied the cruel order of Pharaoh. Her natural devotion to her child seems to have been intensified by his extraordinary beauty. She could not believe it was the will of God that such a child should perish. When she no longer could hide the babe in her home, she wove a basket of papyrus, coverd it with pitch to make it water tight, placed her child in it and set the little vessel afloat amid the reeds near the bank of the Nile. The place she selected was that where the daughter of Pharaoh came daily to bathe. She stationed Miriam, the older sister of the babe, near enough to see what might happen. When the princess reaches the bank of the river she discovers the little ark. As the cover is removed the babe weeps, possibly startled at the sight of strange faces.

The pitiful cry touches the heart of the princess, and she recognizes the child as a Hebrew babe who has been condemned to die. Miriam, probably noting the look of sympathy, makes her shrewd proposal: "Shall I go and call to thee a nurse of the Hebrew women, that she may nurse the child for thee? And Pharaoh's daughter said to her, Go. And the maid went and called the child's mother. And Pharaoh's daughter said unto her, Take the child away and nurse it for me, and I will give thee thy wages. And the woman took the child and nursed it." It had been a venture of faith, and this faith had been richly rewarded. Not only was the child saved, but returned to its mother, who was promised wages for nursing her own babe. In process of time the child was brought to the palace and known as the son of Pharaoh's daughter. By her he was named Moses ("Drawn-forth") as she recalled his rescue from death.

Thus faith is not inaction. Nor is its source found only in sentiment or in selfish desire. There were promises of deliverance. The predicted years of Egyptian bondage were running out. What hopes sprang from such predictions cannot be affirmed. Certain it is that these parents of Moses trusted in God, acted with wisdom and courage, and risked their lives to save the life of their child. Their faith is the more remarkable in view of the idolatry which had overtaken so large a portion of the people. Yet it is out of such believing remnants that God ever has been bringing to pass His saving purpose.

Today, in all lands, countless children are in peril, threatened with physical and moral and spiritual death. Their cries may not be articulate; but when they reach sympathetic hearts, when intelligent effort is put forth, when faith in God is exercised by parents and friends and loyal servants of the King, precious lives are preserved and leaders and deliverers are provided to meet the deepest needs of mankind.

His Preparation. (Ch. 2:11-25). When God plans to accomplish a great work for the world He usually selects a man of conspicuous talents, whom He carefully trains for the task. This is not always so. Sometimes those are chosen who, according to human standards, are "ignorant and unlearned men." However, in the case of Moses his education was as extraordinary as his subsequent career. His training was divided into three periods: first, in the home of his parents, then at the court of the king, and then in the desert of Midian.

Just how long he remained under the care of his mother, it is difficult to learn, nor is it known what associations with his parents were continued after he was taken from his humble home. It is absolutely certain, however, that the first period of his training was most important of all. Then it was that he was taught those great truths which were the firm and abiding foundation of his character. From those believing parents he learned the great traditions of his ancestors which are recorded in the book of Genesis. He was made familiar with the pitiful state of his fellow Hebrews. He was pointed to the great future prophesied and promised to his race. His earliest impressions were of faith in God, of dependence upon His power, of the necessity of obeying His will.

It is impossible to estimate the value and the enduring influence of early impressions made upon the mind of a child. The religious education of the young cannot be begun too early; it is the chief factor in molding a character and a career. Such training was of importance in the case of Moses, for, with the exception of Christ, he was to be the unrivalled spiritual leader of the human race. It is to him the origin of Judaism, and also of Christianity, and of Islam can be traced.

The second period of his training began at a very early age. The scene was the palace of the king. He was known as the son of Pharaoh's daughter. "He was learned in all the wisdom of the Egyptians" (Acts 7:22), and this at a time when the marvelous civilization of Egypt was at its height and was unsurpassed by that of any nation in the world. He was given the education befitting a prince, acquainting him with literary forms, with legal procedure, with political and economic problems, and with the symbolism of religious worship. The statement of Stephen that he was "mighty in words and in deeds" has been interpreted to mean that he was eminent as a statesman and a soldier. Such, indeed, are the traditions by which his exploits are glorified. Surely his training was fitting him for his great task of guiding and organizing his people.

Thus these two periods of training were invaluable. Moses knew his people Israel, its origin, its pitiful bondage, its promises of glory; this he had learned from his parents. He also knew the oppressor, all the power, the pride, the cruelty of Egypt. Yet he needed a third period of training; this was to be in the school of failure, of exile, of loneliness, of deep meditation, of communion with God.

When forty years of age he made his great renunciation. He determined to give up the glories of the court, even the possible grandeur of a throne, and to ally himself with a race of slaves, hoping to become their leader and deliverer. "By faith Moses, when he was come to years, refused to be called the son of Pharaoh's daughter; choosing rather to suffer affliction with the people of God, than to enjoy the pleasures of sin for a season" (Heb. 11:24, 25). His faith appeared in his regarding the enslaved Hebrews as the chosen "people of God," and in believing the divine promises of their release and of their future blessing to the world. This led him to choose humiliation and distress rather than for a time to enjoy "the pleasure of sin." This latter does not refer to possible sensual and unlawful gratifications, but to the continued acceptance of royal favor and all the delights of princely position and power afforded him by the oppressor of his people, instead of serving as their deliverer. The "sin" would have been that of being disloyal to them and untrue to his divinely appointed task.

By faith he made such a choice "accounting the reproach of Christ greater riches than the treasures of Egypt" (Heb. 11:26). The reproach he endured was involved in his believing and acting on the promises of God, which found their ultimate fulfillment in Christ of whom Moses was himself a type as a suffering saviour.

This decision was one of almost matchless heroism. However, his new course was begun with an act of such rashness and self-confidence as to indicate his need of a further period of discipline and development before his life task could be undertaken.

As he "went out" and looked on the pitiful condition of "his brethren," he was filled with compassion,

which soon blazed into indignation as he saw a cruel
Egyptian taskmaster scourging a helpless, bleeding Hebrew. Looking about to be sure there was no observer,
he killed the brutal oppressor, dragged away the body
and buried it in the sand. This deed of Moses is not to
be defended. The Egyptian was hardly deserving of
death, and, in any case, Moses held no office warranting
him to pronounce a sentence or to inflict a penalty. The
provocation was great, the motive was sympathy, yet
the act was hasty, passionate, self-willed, presumptuous.
The result was to postpone for forty years the beginning
of his notable career.

The very next day, or soon after, when attempt-
ing to reconcile two of his own race, he was startled to
receive the insolent rebuke: "Who made thee a ruler
and a judge over us? Intendest thou to kill me as thou
killest the Egyptian?" Moses was deeply distressed by
such ingratitude. He was keenly disappointed, "For he
supposed his brethren would have understood how that
God by his hand would deliver them: but they understood not" (Acts 7:25).

Furthermore, Moses was alarmed that his rash
act was known; and when he heard that the report had
reached the king and that Pharaoh was demanding his
death, he fled from Egypt and hid in the land of Midian,
on the southeastern coast of the peninsula of Sinai.

His people were not without fault; and in the
providence of God "this Moses whom they refused, saying, Who made thee a ruler and a judge? the same did
God send to be a ruler and a deliverer" (Acts 7:35). For
this immortal work Moses was finally prepared by his
stay in Midian.

His first experience in this strange land has an aspect of romance. He gave chivalrous help to the seven daughters of Jethro, the priest of Midian. They were being troubled by insolent shepherds, who were preventing them from watering their flocks. In gratitude Jethro extended to Moses generous hospitality, offered him employment, and ultimately gave to him Zipporah his daughter in marriage. If this was romance, it was none the less pathetic. He whose companions had been courtiers, he who might have married some Egyptian princess, was now the husband of a simple shepherdess who shared none of his culture, his tastes, his memories, or his dreams. There is nostalgia in the very name given to his firstborn son. He called him Gershom, "for he said, I have been a *stranger* in a strange land" (Ch. 2:22). This marriage was a symbol of the life he lived for forty years, caring for sheep, in the deserts of Midian. Yet thus he was being trained to be the great shepherd of his people Israel. In that same region he was to guide and sustain and discipline this people, during their forty years of journeying. Now he was becoming familiar with the roads, the resources, the climate, the conditions of life of this land, and was intimately related to Jethro, a man of great prominence, who later on was to be of real assistance to him in his task (Ch. 18). Most important of all, here in the vast solitudes, here under the skies and the silent stars, here during long days of loneliness and meditation, he came to understand himself and to know God.

He had never forgotten his people in Egypt. Nor had God forgotten them. "God heard their groaning, and God remembered his covenant with Abraham, with

Isaac, and with Jacob. And God looked upon the children of Israel, and God had respect unto them." He was shaping His instrument. He was training in Midian the deliverer who was to lead them out of "the house of bondage."

His Call. (Chs. 3:1 to 4:17). In his earlier years Moses had come to believe that he was to be the deliverer of Israel. An act of rash self-confidence had resulted in a long period of exile and inaction and discipline. Not until he was eighty years old did he receive the divine summons to his task.

The story of his call is instructive and inspiring. It is an illustration of the truth that "every man's life is a plan of God," and it is an encouragement also as we undertake the work of each succeeding day.

The scene is laid under the very shadow of Sinai, or Horeb, on the summit of which mountain Moses afterwards received the Law, and at the base of which the Covenant was formed which made Israel a nation with Jehovah as king. For forty years Moses had been serving as a humble shepherd. On this memorable day he had led the flock to the western border of the wilderness. Farther to the west, a three days' journey, lay Egypt. Possibly Moses was thinking of his brethren in their bitter bondage. Suddenly he saw a bush, a cluster of dry shrubs, ablaze with fire, but unconsumed. "Out of the midst of the bush" came the voice of God calling Moses by name. This "burning bush" has been taken ever as a symbol of the people of God, of Israel in bondage but not destroyed, of the church in the fires of persecution but flourishing still—*ardens sed virens.* The burning bush is a familiar emblem, as is the motto associated with it, *Nec tamen consumebatur*, "Yet it was not consumed."

Possibly, too, Moses saw here an object lesson of the truth God wished him to learn; he was like the insignificant thorn bush, but God was to be in him, and with him; infinite strength would be dwelling in utter weakness.

It was in this story of the burning bush that our Lord Jesus found embedded the message of eternal hope. If God was the God of Abraham and Isaac and Jacob, then even death could not destroy those who belonged to Him. His people are assured of resurrection and heavenly life (Mark 12:26, 27).

There are those who believe that the divine appearance in the Bush, "the angel of the Lord," was actually an appearance of Christ. It is enough to conclude that the phrase expresses God in the act of self-manifestation, by whatever means He was revealed. The voice which came from the bush was the voice of the Lord. Moses realized that he was in the divine presence. He heard the solemn command: "Draw not nigh hither; put off thy shoes from off thy feet, for the place whereon thous standest is holy ground" (Ch. 3:5). The place where God manifests Himself is always holy. It should be approached and regarded with reverence. In the Orient the removal of the sandals or shoes is still required on entering a place of worship. It is a symbolic act representing the removal of the uncleanness caused by contact with the world. Holiness is required of those who worship a holy God.

Moses showed his reverence by covering his face: "He was afraid to look upon God" (Ch. 3:6).

Then came the divine revelation and the clear call to action: "And the Lord said, I have surely seen the affliction of my people which are in Egypt, and have heard their cry by reason of their taskmasters; for I know their sorrows; and I am come down to deliver them out of the hand of the Egyptians, and to bring them up out of that land unto a good land and a large, unto a land flowing with milk and honey. . . . Come now therefore, and I will send thee unto Pharaoh, that thou mayest bring forth my people the children of Israel out of Egypt" (Ch. 3:7-10).

Moses is startled. He shrinks back with the cry: "Who am I, that I should go unto Pharaoh, and that I should bring forth the children of Israel out of Egypt?" What a contrast with the Moses of other years, no longer bold, impetuous, impatient, but timid, hesitant, diffident. As a young nobleman at the court of the king he seemed to feel quite equal to the task of delivering his people, and rashly smites one of their oppressors. Now, during those long years of loneliness in the wilderness, he had learned his own limitations and weakness. In real humility he exclaims, "Who am I?" Yet he was truly prepared for this task. He had great genius and marked talents. He had been disciplined in the court and in the wilderness. God had chosen and trained His instrument. Lack of self-confidence was a real condition of success, if only Moses now would trust in God.

So there comes the divine reply: "Certainly I will be with thee." That is the blessed assurance which has strengthened the chosen servants of God through all the ages. It is the very word of the Master as He sends out His messengers to witness for him: "Lo, I am with you alway, even unto the end of the world."

For Moses another word of assurance is added: "And this shall be a token unto thee, that I have sent thee: When thou hast brought forth the people out of Egypt, ye shall serve God upon this mountain." This token was still in the future. The present demanded faith. However, the promise that the people could be brought to Sinai, there to worship God, was an assurance that all intervening obstacles would be removed. Although Moses felt himself inadequate to the task, he should believe that the choice of God must be a wise choice, and that God was really committed to supply all needed guidance and wisdom and strength.

However, Moses is not satisfied: "Behold, when I come unto the children of Israel, and shall say unto them, The God of your fathers hath sent me unto you; and they shall say unto me, What is his name? *What shall I say unto them?*" This is the question that meets every public servant of God: What shall I say? and the answer is this: Tell your hearers about God. Speak of His nature, His mercy, His love, His redeeming grace.

More specifically, however, Moses wished to know what to say about the character of God: "What is his name?" Then came the significant mysterious answer: "I AM THAT I AM: and he said: Thus shalt thou say unto the children of Israel, I AM hath sent me unto you."

The "name" denotes revealed character. The words "I AM" indicate absolute and essential being. They declare that God is a Person, that He is self-ex-

istent, changeless, eternal. He is not the creation of
man's fancy. He is not "that stream of tendencies which
makes for righteousness." He is not "the sum of things,"
or merely "the soul of the universe." He is the only
reality, the only independent Being. There are some
scholars who prefer to translate the words I AM as
future, I WILL BE. The name would then indicate not
merely the nature of God but His relation to His people. He is the One who is to act. He is the Deliverer,
the Redeeming God. Others interpret the phrase as
"He who causes to be," that is, the Creator. In every
case, the message to Israel was to be that Moses has
come as the messenger of a personal, omnipotent God,
who did not sit impassive in the distant heavens, but was
One who cared for His people, who heard their cries,
who was to be their Saviour. In such a God they could
put their trust and they could accept Moses as His
chosen messenger.

God further encouraged Moses by giving him specific directions as to how he was to begin his work. First
of all, he was to gather the "elders" or representatives
of the tribes and to make plain to them his mission and
the promises of God. Then with them he was to approach the King of Egypt with this request: "The Lord
God of the Hebrews has met with us: and now let us
go, we beseech thee, three days' journey into the wilderness, that we may sacrifice to the Lord our God" (Ch.
3:18). There was to be no violence, no insurrection,
only this reasonable request. It was to be a fair test of
the spirit of Pharaoh. If he should grant it, the people
would return to Egypt strengthened, united, and better
prepared for deliverance. If, as was most certain, the re-

quest should be denied, then it would be the more evident that a divine intervention would be necessary. It was expected that Pharaoh would not yield, "not by a mighty hand," that is, under the most severe discipline. Therefore, the promise was added, "I will stretch out my hand and will smite Egypt with all my wonders which I will do in the midst thereof: and after that he will let you go." Nor was there anything dishonest in the further direction to Moses and the elders: "Ye shall not go empty, but every woman shall *borrow* of her neighbor . . . jewels of silver, and jewels of gold, . . . and ye shall spoil the Egyptians." The word "borrow" is a most unfortunate translation and has caused endless cavil and criticism. It is the word usually rendered *"ask,"* and, as the history records, when the last plague had broken the hearts of the Egyptians, they were eager to have the Israelites depart, and gave them anything they requested or desired.

All these instructions to Moses were explicit. He knew just how to proceed, yet he was reluctant to obey the call. He had a third objection: "They *will not believe me*, nor hearken unto my voice: for they will say, The Lord hath not appeared unto thee" (Ch. 4:1). He lacked credentials. Therefore in grace God promised him the power to work miracles, and miracles in sacred history are usually wrought with the definite purpose of authenticating a divine mission or accrediting a divinely appointed messenger. Thus Moses was commanded to cast upon the ground his rod, probably his shepherd's staff, "and it became a serpent, and Moses fled before it," and again at the divine command "he put forth his hand, and caught it, and it became a rod in his hand."

Again he was bidden to put his hand into his bosom, "and when he took it out, behold his hand was leprous as snow"; then putting his hand into his bosom and bringing it out "it was turned again as his other flesh." These wonders were to be wrought as signs to the people of Israel, "that they may believe that the Lord God of their fathers . . . hath appeared unto thee." If these two miracles would not convince the people of Moses' divine appointment, he was to work a third: he was to take water from the Nile, which would become blood as he poured it on the ground. These marvels are commonly interpreted as symbols, as well as signs of divine power. The simple rod of the shepherd was to become a power of destruction, and was to be more potent than the scepter of the king. The leprous hand pictured the power to inflict the most dreaded punishment, and the power also to heal and to save. So, too, the water of the sacred Nile might be transformed into the very symbol of death. However interpreted, these miracles were evidently designed to encourage Moses and to accredit him as the messenger of God.

Yet Moses still hesitated to heed the call. "And Moses said unto the Lord, O my Lord, *I am not eloquent*, neither heretofore, nor since thou hast spoken unto thy servant: but I am slow of speech, and of a slow tongue" (Ch. 4:10). This did not imply that Moses had an impediment in his speech, as some have supposed, or that he had forgotten his Egyptian culture, but that he doubted his ability to speak so persuasively as to enlist the following of his people or to move the heart of Pharaoh. "And the Lord said unto him, Who hath made man's mouth? . . . Now therefore go, and I will be with thy mouth, and teach thee what thou shalt say." It would seem that such an assurance would have been sufficient, but Moses is obdurate. His diffidence seems to have developed into stubbornness. He will not be persuaded to undertake the proffered task. "And he said, O my Lord, send, I pray thee, by the hand of him whom thou wilt send." He seems to say, "Send any one you choose, but do not send me." At least he means this: If absolutely necessary, if there is no one else, I will go, but I am sure there must be some better choice.

No wonder we read that "the anger of the Lord was kindled against him." God expressed His divine displeasure. There was nothing of passion or unkindness in the divine mind. God still acted in grace and love. He did not revoke Moses' commission, He did not deny to Moses his glorious task, but He sent another servant to share the responsibility and the honor which had been offered Moses. And the Lord said: "Is not Aaron the Levite thy brother? I know that he can speak well. And also, behold, he cometh forth to meet thee: and when he seeth thee, he will be glad in his heart. And thou shalt speak unto him, and put words in his mouth: and I will be with thy mouth, and with his mouth, and teach you what ye should say . . . and thou shalt be to him instead of God. And thou shalt take this rod in thine hand, wherewith thou shalt do signs" (Ch. 4:14-17).

The rod, the symbol of power, was still to be in the hand of Moses; but the word, the message of God, was to be in the mouth of Aaron. It should be noted that the promise of the sympathy and companionship of a brother did what the promises of the presence of God failed to do. Moses was willing to undertake the task. It also should be noted that Moses had never hesitated for fear of personal harm or loss; he feared that he might fail, and his failure would involve the destiny of his people Israel. His timidity should have been overcome by trust in God. "Humility without faith is too timorous; faith without humility is too hasty." This described the reluctance of Moses now to heed the call of God, as it explains his failure forty years before. It is not humility to refuse the place which God assigns. Rather, it is inordinate timidity born of unbelief.

Aaron did become the helper and companion Moses needed. But who can say that the hesitation of Moses did not have serious consequences? Aaron was the weaker character of the two. He was persuaded in an hour of crisis to make for the people a golden calf as an object of worship, and so disaster was brought upon Israel. It might have been better had Moses responded at once to the call of God. His reluctance led to the appointment of one of less real ability and strength. It is dangerous to decline a task which God assigns. We may feel our inadequacy, but shall we be guilty of letting the work fall into even weaker hands? However, Moses and Aaron do go forward together, each encouraged by the sympathy and affection of the other, and both supported by an unconquerable faith in God. The rod was in the hand of the great deliverer and this humble instrument became the symbol of divine power, the power which set God's people free.

The Apparent Failure. (Chs. 4:18 to 7:7). To meet with defeat as one enters upon his career is discouraging, yet sometimes the results are of abiding value. Such was the experience of Moses in his first appearance before Pharaoh.

However, three incidents are recorded as worthy of note while Moses is still in Midian.

First of all, when he returns to his father-in-law, according to Oriental courtesy, to obtain permission to leave the home, and when he is starting for Egypt with his wife and children, he receives a repetition of his call, an assurance that his enemies in Egypt are dead, and a specific message to Pharaoh: "Thus saith the Lord, Israel is my son, even my firstborn: and I say unto thee, Let my son go that he may serve me, and if thou refuse to let him go, behold I will slay thy son, even thy first-born." So it is when one obeys God, and enters upon the path of duty, he becomes more certain that he is being divinely led, and clearer light cheers him on his way (Ch. 4:18-23).

Then occurs a mysterious and fateful experience. Moses is afflicted with what seems to have been an illness which threatened his life. His wife reluctantly performs upon her infant son a neglected religious rite which was regarded as a seal of the covenant of God with His people. The life of Moses is spared, and his wife and children return to the home of her parents, to remain until Moses comes again from Egypt as the great deliverer. So God requires perfect obedience on the part of all who are enlisted in His service (Ch. 4:24-26).

The third incident is the glad reunion of Moses and Aaron as they meet at the foot of Sinai and rehearse their experiences of the forty years since they were together in Egypt. More important still was their counsel as to how they could fulfill their great mission and be used of God to accomplish His promised deliverance of Israel (Ch. 4:27, 28).

On their arrival in Egypt the brothers call a conference of the "elders," or representatives, of the tribes, and then apparently an assembly of the people. Moved by the eloquence of Aaron and the encouraging signs, the people are persuaded to accept Moses and Aaron as their divinely appointed leaders. They believe the promise of deliverance and they unite in a service of worship and grateful praise. It would have been futile to appeal to the king for release, unless the people were first made one in belief, in purpose and in hope; as today only a united church can make a true approach to an unbelieving world (Ch. 4:29-31).

It required heroic courage and faith on the part of Moses and Aaron to appear before Pharaoh. Pharaoh was a despot of unlimited power, cruel, arrogant, proud, regarding himself as equal to the gods of Egypt. The message of Moses was brief and startling: "Thus saith the Lord God of Israel, Let my people go, that they may hold a feast unto me in the wilderness." The request was reasonable. In obedience to their God, the weary people, might expect to be allowed a brief respite for a religious festival. The place of the observance would be properly at some distance from the Egyptians, to whom animal sacrifices were abhorrent. To them the animals which were to be offered were sacred. A place "three days' journey" distant would avoid needless offence.

The request, however, was in the form of a command. In his reply Pharaoh indicates his wounded pride and anger: "Who is the Lord, that I should obey his voice? . . . I know not the Lord, neither will I let Israel go." Moses and Aaron repeat their request in a somewhat milder form, appealing to the mercy of Pharaoh, who is not asked to "obey" a strange deity, but to allow his captive people to heed the voice of their own God.

The king interprets the request as an attempt on the part of Moses and Aaron to take the people from their tasks, and adds the bitter taunt to Moses and Aaron: "Get you unto your burdens," take your part in the toil of the brick kilns with the rest of the Hebrew slaves.

The refusal of the request was not surprising, but the result filled the suppliants with dismay. A royal command went forth to the effect that the laborers were to be given no more straw but were to make daily the same number of bricks. In his great building operations Pharaoh used bricks made of mud from the Nile mixed with chopped straw to give consistency. When such straw was no longer provided, the people scattered through the country, searching for substitutes in the way of stubble or roots or twigs or dry weeds. With their efforts thus divided, it became impossible to produce the former number of bricks, and as they failed they were cruelly scourged by taskmasters, beneath whose bloody lashes they fainted and died. Thus "bricks without straw" has become a proverbial description of a task which is intolerable or impossible (Ch. 5:1-14).

In their anguish the people appealed directly to the king, ignoring Moses and Aaron. However, Pharaoh only repeats his former heartless charge: "Ye are idle, ye are idle; therefore ye say, Let us go and do sacrifice to the Lord. Go therefore now, and work; for there shall no straw be given you." As the representatives of the people retreated in despair from the audience chamber of the king, they passed Moses and Aaron and reproached them as being responsible for their hopeless plight (Ch. 5:15-21).

It is easy to imagine the distress of soul suffered by Moses. His mission has brought no relief to the people, but has resulted in deeper tragedy. There is only one place to which one can go in such an hour of darkness, only one Person whose word can bring relief: "And Moses returned unto the Lord, and said, Lord, wherefore hast thou so evil entreated this people? Why is it that thou hast sent me? For since I came to Pharaoh to speak in thy name, he hath done evil to this people; neither hast thou delivered thy people at all (Ch. 5:22, 23).

Then came the word of divine comfort and cheer: "Now shalt thou see what I will do to Pharaoh, for with a strong hand he shall let them go and with a strong hand shall he drive them out of his land." Moses has complained of delay. God replies that delay shall continue no longer. The work of deliverance is now to begin. The "strong hand" of the Lord will be so laid upon Pharaoh that he will be eager to have the people leave his land.

Further encouragement is given to the disheartened leader by a reference to the divine name. God promises to reveal himself as being all that this name implies: "And God spake unto Moses, and said unto him, I am JEHOVAH; and I appeared unto Abraham, unto Isaac, and unto Jacob, by the name of EL SHADDAI (God Almighty) but by my name JEHOVAH was

I not known unto them." The patriarchs had known
the name, but to them its full import had not been revealed. "El Shaddai" denotes a God of overpowering
might, and it had brought to the patriarchs the comfort which comes from the assurance of divine power
and possible protection; but "Jehovah" is the God of
revelation and grace, the God who is in covenant relation with his people, the God who dwells with them,
who guides, delivers; who receives their worship and
their praise. Two reasons are given for this promise
made to Moses, one is God's covenant made with the
patriarchs; the other is the sympathy felt for their suffering descendants: "And I have also heard the groaning of the children of Israel . . . and I have remembered
my covenant."

With a message of divine comfort and cheer,
Moses is sent back to the people: "I will redeem you
with a stretched out arm. . . . I will take you to me for a
people, and I will be to you a God. . . . I will bring you
in unto the land, concerning the which I did swear to
give it to Abraham, to Isaac, and to Jacob; and I will
give it to you for a heritage: I am the Lord" (Ch. 6:1-8).

It is not strange, however, that this message, reported to the people by Moses, fell on deaf ears. They
had heard from him such golden promises before; but
these had been followed only by deeper misery and distress. "They hearkened not unto Moses for anguish of
spirit, and for cruel bondage." Nor is it surprising that
Moses is not willing to convey a still more difficult word
to Pharaoh. It is not a request for a "three days' journey" within the limits of Egypt, but a demand "that he
let the children of Israel go out of his land." "And

Moses spake before the Lord, saying, Behold the children of Israel have not hearkened unto me; how then
shall Pharaoh hear me, who am of uncircumcised lips?"

Moses is discouraged. His mission has failed.
His efforts for the people have ended in disaster. Yet
out of apparent defeat and calamity there came certain
blessed results. First of all, the issue was now clearly
joined between Pharaoh and Jehovah. It was no more
the request of Moses that Pharaoh was refusing, but the
command of the eternal God. In the second place,
Moses was learning the fickle and thankless character of
the people he had come to deliver, a people whose re-
bellious and ungrateful spirit he was to endure with
patience during the coming years. Then, too, this very
people were being prepared for their deliverance; searching for stubble, they were becoming accustomed to ab-
sence from their homes; by the increasing bitterness of
their lot, they were being weaned from Egypt; by their
common suffering, they were being more closely bound
together; finding that no relief could be expected from
Pharaoh, they were taught to look for help to God.
Thus out of failure and disaster God was bringing abiding good (Ch. 6:9-12).

As the story of Exodus now turns from defeat to
glorious victory there is introduced, with apparent
abruptness, the genealogy of Moses and Aaron. This is
no interruption. It is a touch of Oriental literary art.
Just before an account of the exploits of the great heroes,
the readers are informed as to who they are, what is
their origin, their pedigree, their descent. The genealogy
is not complete. It is a summary account of the families
of these two brothers. Reuben and Simeon are men-

tioned first, to indicate the place of Levi as third in order among the sons of Jacob. In this record the word "sons" is not always to be taken literally but may indicate "grandsons" or "descendants." The list of names concludes with this statement, showing the purpose of the record: "These are that Aaron and Moses, to whom the Lord said, Bring out the children of Israel from the land of Egypt. . . . These are they which spake to Pharaoh king of Egypt, to bring out the children of Israel from Egypt: these are that Moses and Aaron" (Ch. 6:13-27).

A second paragraph is added before the account of the great deliverance is begun. It renews the commission of Moses and Aaron: they are to demand that Pharaoh shall release Israel. It repeats the prediction that Pharaoh will refuse: "I will harden Pharaoh's heart" (Ch. 4:21). This last phrase has been the occasion of endless controversy and of real perplexity. Much relief is found in the definite record that Pharaoh hardened his own heart (Chs. 8:15, 32; 9:34). There is no real contradiction. The divine and the human processes are one. Pharaoh was unwilling to obey God, and with every new appeal he became more stubborn and defiant. God sent these appeals and emphasized them by new signs, and thus it could be said that he was hardening Pharaoh's heart. This was the operation of a natural law by which God works. Every act of disobedience makes it more difficult for one to obey. The statement as to Pharaoh should be regarded as a solemn warning to every reader rather than as a subject for controversy and debate.

This paragraph further emphasizes the prediction

that the divine signs and wonders by which Pharaoh's heart was to be hardened will result, however, in the deliverance of Israel. By these "judgments" the Egyptians will learn the real character of the Lord: "And the Egyptians shall know that I am the Lord when I stretch forth my hand upon Egypt, and bring out the children of Israel from among them."

This renewed commission Moses and Aaron accept. The hesitation of Moses is ended. He goes forward without fear and boldly undertakes his difficult task. Triumph is now to begin. "And Moses and Aaron did as the Lord commanded them, so did they." The time for action has come. A last introductory line is added: "And Moses was fourscore years old, and Aaron fourscore and three years old, when they spake unto Pharaoh" (Ch. 7:7).

THE PLAGUES OF EGYPT. [Chs. 7:8 to 11:10.]

Two of the names employed to describe the plagues visited upon the Egyptians are "signs" and "judgments." The first indicates credentials intended to prove the mission of Moses as the representative of Jehovah; the second indicates that the miracles were wrought as punishments designed to break the hard heart of Pharaoh.

The plagues were all closely related to natural phenomena; their supernatural character was indicated by their appearance and disappearance at the word of Moses, by their extent and severity and by their rapid succession. The natural objects involved were sacred to the gods of Egypt and the plagues indicated the impotence of these deities. However, the real struggle was not between the gods of Egypt and the God of Israel, but between Jehovah and Pharaoh, between the God of heaven and the king of Egypt.

The rhythmic and climactic order of the plagues has often been noted. They form three groups of three plagues each, followed by the final dread blow, the "death of the first born." The first of each group is introduced by a warning to Pharaoh; the last of each group is inflicted without warning. The third plague marks the defeat of the magicians, the sixth manifests their inability longer to stand before the king, the ninth is followed by the final separation of Moses and Pharaoh. The first three are loathsome—blood-stained waters, frogs, and lice; the second are painful—stinging flies, murrain on the beasts, boils on the Egyptians; the last three are appalling—hail, locusts, and darkness; the tenth is overwhelming—death enters every home. After the record of the first three plagues, mention is made of the fact that the children of Israel, in the land of Goshen, have been immune. After the next three plagues, the Egyptians are warned to seek places of protection. Before the tenth plague, it was announced that none of the people of Pharaoh can escape. It is a sad story of suffering and distress, but it seems that in no other way could the stubborn willfulness of the king be overcome: only by such calamities could deliverance be wrought for the people of God.

Before the narrative of the plagues begins, it is recorded that Pharaoh requested Moses to perform a miracle in his presence. Probably he had heard of the miracles wrought by Aaron before the people (Ch. 4:30) and was moved by curiosity, or he wished to show that any work of Moses could be equalled or surpassed by the skill of his own magicians. At the word of Moses, Aaron casts down his rod, which at once becomes a serpent. The magicians do the same with their rods, probably by some sleight-of-hand or juggler's trick. The contrast became obvious, however, when "Aaron's rod swallowed up their rods." The defeat of the magicians, however, had the effect only of making the king more stubborn in his refusal to grant the request of Moses. We read, "He hardened Pharaoh's heart." This is an unfortunate translation. "Pharaoh's heart hardened itself" would be a better rendering of the words, as, indeed, the next verse states: "And the Lord said unto Moses, Pharaoh's heart is hardened, he refuseth to let the people go." In the beginning of the contest it should be noted that Pharaoh hardened his own heart, and, later, by a perfectly natural process, God hardened the heart of Pharaoh as He made His successive appeals to the king by the lips of Aaron and by the miracles of Moses (Ch. 7:8-13).

The *first plague* involved the waters of the worshipped Nile. After a personal appeal to Pharaoh and a solemn warning, in case he refused to let the people go, Aaron "lifted up the rod, and smote the waters that were in the river, in the sight of Pharaoh, and in the sight of his servants; and all the waters that were in the river were turned to blood." This not only discredited the Nile god, it was a severe physical affliction. Not only did the water become red in color, which might occur at a certain season of the year, but it had the appearance and qualities of blood. That the plague was no mere natural occurrence is evident from the suddenness of the change, its immediate connection with the rod of Moses, and from the terrible effect. The fish died, and the people sustained life only by digging hasty wells, which supplied brackish water. "And the magicians of Egypt did so with their enchantments," but this must have been a poor and petty performance, with the little water at their command, and in view of the many possibilities of deception and trickery. However, Pharaoh seemed satisfied and sullenly returned to his palace. It is recorded again that his "heart was hardened" (Ch. 7:14-25).

The *second plague* was loathsome. Again the divine command had come to Pharaoh, again he had been warned of disaster, again he had proved obdurate. Then "Aaron stretched out his hand over the waters of Egypt, and the frogs came up and covered the land of Egypt." They appeared in such incredible numbers that they infested houses and bedchambers, polluted cooking utensils, and defiled the water and the food. They were regarded sacred and could not be killed, yet one could not move without stepping on them. They were hideous to the eye, maddening to the ear, sickening to the touch. The suffering of the people was intolerable; even the heart of Pharaoh was moved. The magicians attempted some weak imitation of the work of Moses and Aaron, but the king was desperate. He called for Moses and Aaron, and said, "Intreat the Lord that he may take away the frogs from me, and from my people, and I will let the people go, that they may do sacrifice unto the Lord."

The words of Moses, "Glory over me: when shall I intreat for thee?" are not quite clear. Probably he means: "I submit to thy will" or "I am content to do thy bidding; what time shall I mention in my prayer to God for relief?" Pharaoh replies: "Tomorrow." Moses promises that the request will be fulfilled, but he is not satisfied, in that the king simply recognizes Jehovah (vs. 8) but insists that he must admit "that there is none like unto the Lord our God." In answer to the prayer of Moses and Aaron, God removes the plague. The frogs die. However, the land is filled with the horror of their decaying bodies. "But when Pharaoh saw there was respite, he hardened his heart." He exerted all the power of his will to continue his disobedience to the will of God (Ch. 8:1-15).

The *third plague* came unannounced. It was a judgment upon Pharaoh for having broken his promise and having hardened his heart. He was given no choice of yielding before the blow fell. It came in the form of lice which swarmed from the dust in every part of the land and became a torment "upon man and upon beast." Some have supposed that the plague consisted of mosquitoes or of sand flies or fleas. However, the usual translation is probably correct. The disaster comes from the ground, which was regarded as sacred, as the first two plagues had their source in the waters of the worshipped Nile. The magicians were baffled in their attempts to reproduce the miracle; they had been given no time to prepare and any attempt at imitation would have been difficult. They admitted to Pharaoh that this plague must be the work of some god. Yet Pharaoh would not be warned. His "heart was hardened, and he harkened not unto them" (Ch. 8:18-19).

The *fourth plague* was "flies." The exact nature

of these insects is uncertain. Possibly they were beetles, which were reverenced by the Egyptians as symbols of life. They were injurious, however, not only to the human body but to the furniture of houses and to the crops in the fields. Moses warned Pharaoh that this scourge was to fall and added a divine prediction which indicated its supernatural character: "I will sever in that day the land of Goshen, in which my people dwell; that no swarms of flies shall be there; to the end thou mayest know that I am the Lord in the midst of the earth." Yet Pharaoh would not be warned. The plague fell with all its terror and the whole country was desolated. The king suffered bitterly, as did all his subjects. In consternation, he sends for Moses and Aaron. Pretending to yield he gives this limited permission: "Go ye, sacrifice to your God in the land." Moses replies that such a festival would be impossible "in the land," because the sacrifice of animals regarded as sacred would be an intolerable offense and abomination to the Egyptians; the people must go, as requested, a "three days' journey into the wilderness." Pharaoh is helpless. He modifies his restriction with the words: "Only ye shall not go very far away." Moses promises to ask the Lord for relief but warns Pharaoh not to "deal deceitfully any more in not letting the people go." However, as soon as the plague has been removed with miraculous swiftness, "Pharaoh hardened his heart at this time also, neither would he let the people go." In spite of the deep impression, and in direct conflict with his promise, Pharaoh again hardens his own heart (Ch. 8:20-32).

The *fifth plague* involved a disastrous loss of property. It fell upon the "cattle," in which the wealth of the Egyptians largely consisted; "upon horses, upon the asses, upon the camels, upon the oxen, and upon the sheep." It was in the form of a "murrain," from which dread diseases "all the cattle of Egypt died." Pharaoh had been warned, and had been told that from this destruction the cattle of the children of Israel would be spared. The king did not believe that such a miracle of preservation could be possible. He sent messengers to Goshen, who returned with the report that "there was not one of the cattle of the Israelites dead." Yet Pharaoh was unmoved. His "heart was hardened and he did not let the people go" (Ch. 9:1-7).

The *sixth plague* marks a change in the nature of the judgments. For the first time the persons of the Egyptians are severely and bitterly attacked. Moses and Aaron scattered ashes toward heaven, as a possible challenge to the false gods of Egypt, and as a symbol of the widespread suffering which was to be visited upon the people. Then, we read, "It became a boil breaking forth with blains upon man, and upon beast." These "burning tumors or carbuncles" caused the most exquisite torture. The severity of the plague is attested by the statement that "the magicians could not stand before Moses because of the boils." The infliction was universal, extending even to such cattle as, because they were housed or sheltered, had escaped the previous plague. Still the king was unmoved. Now we read for the first time that "the Lord hardened the heart of Pharaoh." Previously Pharaoh had hardened his own heart; now one who has resisted the divine appeals, and who twice has felt inclined to yield, finds it impossible to relent. By an inner compulsion he is driven onward to meet his own destruction and to bring new disasters upon his people (Ch. 9:8-12).

The *seventh plague* is even more severe. It is preceded by the most solemn warning yet addressed to Pharaoh. He is assured that the judgments of God are not exhausted; others are to be inflicted which will make his hard heart to yield. His life has been spared until now so that the power of God may be more fully shown by the plagues which were to follow. The words of Moses may be translated more accurately as follows: "And now I might have stretched out my hand, and smitten both thee and thy people with pestilence, and then thou hadst been cut off from the earth; but truly on this account have I kept thee alive, that my name may be declared throughout all the earth" (Ch. 9:15-16).

It will be noticed that here, and henceforth, Moses rather than Aaron is the one to speak and to act. Possibly his heroic faith is being rewarded by restoring to him some of the dignity and power which because of his unbelief had been taken from him and given to his brother. God sometimes restores to us what by rash refusal we have lost.

The character of the plague was appalling. Rain storms in Egypt are rare. Now, however, amid crashes of thunder and accompanied by deadly electric disturbances, enormous hail stones were poured upon the land. They were so devastating as to destroy not only crops and trees but every man and beast, excepting those for which shelter had been provided after the warning of Moses. "Only in the land of Goshen, where the children of Israel were, was there no hail."

The spirit of Pharaoh is broken. He confesses

his guilt and pleads for mercy: "I have sinned this time: the Lord is righteous, and I and my people are wicked. Intreat the Lord (for it is enough) that there be no more mighty thunderings and hail; and I will let you go, and ye shall stay no longer." Moses is suspicious of the permanence of the king's repentance. However, he braved the storm and "went out of the city . . . and spread abroad his hands unto the Lord; and the thunder and the hail ceased;" but "when Pharaoh saw that the rain and the hail and the thunder were ceased, he sinned yet more, and hardened his heart. . . . Neither would he let the children of Israel go" (Ch. 9:13-35).

The *eighth plague* was so familiar yet so terrible in its character that when Moses threatened an invasion of locusts, more deadly than ever before known, the councillors of the king plead with him to yield. Pharaoh attempted an impossible compromise. He called for Moses and Aaron and offered to let the men go to the wilderness for the proposed festival, but insisted upon detaining the women and children. When Moses replies that they must go "with our young and with our old . . . with our flocks and with our herds . . . to hold a feast unto the Lord," Moses and Aaron "were driven out from Pharaoh's presence." So the grievous blow fell. "The locusts went up over all the land. . . . They covered the face of the whole earth, so that the land was darkened; and they did eat every herb of the land, and all the fruit of the trees which the hail had left: and there remained not any green thing . . . through all the land of Egypt."

Pharaoh was appalled. He sent in haste for Moses and Aaron and implored them to intercede with the Lord, confessing his sin even more humbly than before. At the request of Moses the plague ceases. The locusts which had been brought by the east wind are now removed by a strong west wind, which drives them into the sea. The locusts and the wind and the sea are all within the sphere of nature, but there is something more than a natural event in a calamity that comes and goes so suddenly at the word of a man, and by its unmatched horror bends the will of the king.

However, "the Lord hardened Pharaoh's heart," as Pharaoh so often had hardened his own heart "so that he would not let the children of Israel go" (Ch. 10:1-20).

The *ninth plague*, like the third and the sixth, comes unannounced. Something of its terror can be imagined from the brief record. "And Moses stretched forth his hand toward heaven; and there was a thick darkness in all the land of Egypt three days: they saw not one another, neither rose any from his place for three days: but all the children of Israel had light in their dwellings." Probably this plague, like the others, had a natural basis. This may have been a sand storm or a fog; but its preternatural character is attested by its suddenness, by its connection with the action of Moses in obedience to a divine command, by its intensity ("a darkness which may be felt") and by its effect on Pharaoh. He worshipped the sun god. No such visitation ever had been known in all the history of Egypt. In alarm and consternation the king summons Moses and consents to let the people go. However, they must leave their cattle in Egypt. This would assure the return of the Israelites. This compromise Moses rejects absolutely.

The very purpose of the proposed festival is to sacrifice
to the Lord, and it is not yet known what portion of
their cattle the Lord will expect. Pharaoh is disappointed, defeated, enraged. He rudely dismisses Moses
from his presence and threatens him with death if he
returns. "And Moses said, Thou hast spoken well, I will
see thy face again no more." The controversy is over.
Moses leaves the king forever, but not until he first has
pronounced the doom, the coming of the tenth plague,
the death which is to smite the land of Egypt (Ch.
10:24-29).

The *tenth plague* was threatened by Moses after
he had been dismissed by Pharaoh in anger, and while
he still stood in the presence of the king. The story is
interrupted by a brief parenthesis (Ch. 11:1-3) in which
are repeated the promise and the command previously
addressed by the Lord to Moses. The assurance is given
that, after one final, dread visitation, Pharaoh would be
so moved that he would compel the children of Israel to
leave the land in haste. Furthermore, the Egyptians
would be so eager to be rid of the Israelites that they
would gladly give them anything they might "ask."

Most unfortunately, this last word has been translated "borrow." It is the same word used when Sisera
"asked" water, and when Solomon "asked" wisdom.
Nothing of deception or of dishonesty is suggested when
the Israelites asked for jewels of gold and silver and for
raiment. At the most, it was a poor partial payment for
years of cruel and unrequited toil (Ch. 3:22).

The important statement is added: "And the
Lord gave the people favour in the sight of the Egyptians. Moreover the man Moses was very great in the

land of Egypt, in the sight of Pharaoh's servants, and in the sight of the people." This explains the attitude of the people toward the Israelites. They had come to regard Moses as an equal of their king and as a man wielding supernatural power, whose dire predictions had never failed.

As the parenthesis ends (vss. 1-3) and the narrative of Chapter 10 is resumed, Moses announces to Pharaoh the last and most terrible of the plagues. On a certain night, throughout all the land of Egypt, the first-born of every man and beast would die. No harm should come to any of the children of Israel. The Egyptian rulers who stood about Pharaoh as Moses was speaking would be so overwhelmed with grief and terror that they would "bow down themselves" unto Moses and implore him, "saying: Get thee out and all the people that follow thee." "And after that," Moses concluded, "I will go out." Then, for the last time, Moses left the council chamber of the king. He was filled with indignation. The repeated promises of Pharaoh had been broken, the life of Moses was now threatened, he was being dismissed disgracefully, he was denied the right of a future audience. No wonder that "he went out from Pharaoh in a great anger."

This section of the book which records the nine plagues concludes with a brief summary (Ch. 11:9, 10) which states that (1) God had predicted that these plagues would not move the heart of Pharaoh, (2) that this failure would make necessary more punishments, (3) that as a penalty God hardened the heart of Pharaoh after Pharaoh repeatedly had hardened his own heart (Ch. 11:1-10).

THE PASSOVER. [Ch. 12:1-51.]

The supreme chapter in the Book of Exodus is the twelfth. It records the "going out," or "the exodus," which gives to the book its name. It relates the last dread plague which made possible this departure from Egypt. It also describes the festival established to commemorate this great historic deliverance of the children of Israel.

The account opens with the directions given to Moses and Aaron (vss. 1-20) and reported by them to the elders of the people (vss. 21-28), for the observance of the festival, which was to be known as the Feast of the Passover. The central object of the observance was the Paschal lamb. This was to be "without blemish, a male of the first year." It was to be chosen on the tenth day of the month Abib, later known as the month Nisan, and on the fourteenth day, in the early evening, it was to be sacrificed. Henceforth this month was to be regarded as the first month of the sacred year. The blood of the lamb was to be sprinkled on the door posts and the lintel of every house in which the Israelites dwelt. The lamb was to be roasted and eaten with unleavened bread and bitter herbs. It was to be wholly consumed, and if not wholly consumed, the rest was to be burned. Everyone who partook of the feast was to have his "loins girded," his shoes on his feet, his staff in his hand, and to be ready to start on the journey toward the Land of Promise. The feast was to be "the *Lord's Passover*," for this was the divine message: "I will pass through the land of Egypt this night, and will smite all the firstborn in the land of Egypt, both man and beast.

. . . And the blood shall be to you for a token upon the houses where ye are: and *when I see the blood*, I will *pass over you* and the plague shall not be upon you to destroy you, when I smite the land of Egypt. And this day shall be unto you for a memorial; and ye shall keep it a feast . . . by an ordinance for ever (Ch. 12:1-14).

These directions for the observance of Passover were followed by instructions, given at a later period, for the institution of the Feast of Unleavened Bread. The two feasts were so vitally related that these subsequent instructions are properly inserted here (Ch. 12:15-20). For seven days, following the day of the Passover, a glad festival was to be held to symbolize the fellowship of God with His people. However, the main feature was the exclusion from every home of all leaven during the period of the feast. The historic reason for the use of unleavened bread on the night of the Passover was the haste of the departure from Egypt (Ch. 12:39). In later years a symbolic meaning was connected with this prohibition of the use of leaven. As leaven was the symbol of corruption, the intimation was that God would hold fellowship only with a holy people. So closely united were these two feasts that the word "Passover" commonly was understood to include both.

How far the meaning of Passover may have been understood by the Israelites, it is difficult to say. It must have conveyed some definite message of redemption. It commemorated deliverance from death and from bondage. The Israelites knew that they did not escape the plague which fell upon the Egyptians because they were themselves free from fault, but because God graciously had provided for them a way of escape. This way involved the payment of a price. The shed blood of a lamb, symbolizing a life poured out, was the appointed ransom which delivered from death the firstborn in the Hebrew homes on the night when the firstborn of the Egyptians perished. This scourge of Egypt was the final blow which brought deliverance to Israel. It was natural that the feast which commemorated this twofold and completed redemption should have been celebrated as the chief feast of the Hebrew year, and that the calendar was changed to make the month of this observance the first month of the sacred year.

However little Moses and his people may have understood the meaning of their instructions, Moses accepted God's provision for deliverance and trusted in His promise: "Through faith he kept the passover and the sprinkling of blood, lest he that destroyed the firstborn should touch them (Heb. 11:28).

What the Feast of Passover means to the Christian in its symbolic teaching is made clear by the words of Paul: "For even Christ our Passover is sacrificed for us: Therefore let us keep the feast, not with old leaven, neither with the leaven of malice and wickedness; but with the unleavened bread of sincerity and truth" (I Cor. 5:7, 8).

The Christian has been "redeemed . . . from his vain manner of life . . . with the precious blood of Christ, as of a lamb without blemish and without spot" (I Peter 1:18). One is saved through no merit of his own, but only as he identifies himself with Christ, who died for us and rose again and lives forevermore. When one accepts this free salvation, his peace with God and his sense of security depend wholly on his trust in the

promises of God. The transaction is finished. There is
for him "now no condemnation." He is like one seated
at a feast, absolutely safe for time and eternity because
of the blood which has been sprinkled, the blood of the
Lamb. However, he begins now to keep the Feast of
Unleavened Bread. He excludes evil from his life, not in
order to be saved but because he has been saved. Indeed,
his life becomes a "feast," not a fast. The acceptance of
Christ, the experience of peace with God, the assurance
of salvation, the joy of fellowship with a living Lord, the
deliverance from fear and from the bondage of sin, all
mark the beginning of a new life. All former experiences
seem unreal and unsatisfying; Passover has come, "the
beginning of days," the commencement of a sacred year.

The relation of the Feast of Passover to the Supper of our Lord is vital and familiar. The sacrament
commemorates, but does not repeat, the sacrifice which
was offered once for all. In the hour of "communion"
we call to mind the death of Christ for us. We see the
symbols of His broken body and His shed blood. Since
He is our Paschal Lamb we feed upon Him by faith, and
receive new spiritual strength as we realize also that we
are one with our fellow worshippers in the "Assembly of
Israel." We eat bitter herbs of repentance, and we re-
solve to keep more perfectly the Feast of Unleavened
Bread in lives of new purity and holiness. We too are
like the Israelites, for we eat as those who are prepared
for the journey, and we start anew toward the land of
promise. Passover and the Lord's Supper are alike in
this respect: both are related to deliverances that are
past and to greater deliverances yet to come. The Passover pointed back, year after year, to the deliverance

from Egypt, and it pointed forward to the time when its symbols would be fulfilled in the deliverance to be wrought on Calvary. The sacrament points back to that Passover feast when our Lord suffered to secure our redemption, and it points us forward to a still greater deliverance when He shall come to complete our salvation, for as we partake of the bread and the wine we "do shew forth the Lord's death till he come."

When all these instructions for observing the Passover feast had been communicated by Moses to the elders of the people ,"the children of Israel went away, and did as the Lord had commanded" (Ch. 12:4-28).

Then the fatal blow, *the tenth plague*, fell upon Pharaoh and the Egyptians. The tragic event is recorded with startling brevity: "And it came to pass that at midnight, the Lord smote all the firstborn in the land of Egypt, from the firstborn of Pharaoh that sat on his throne unto the firstborn of the captive that was in the dungeon; and all the firstborn of cattle." The natural agency employed may have been a pestilence which swept the land. The miraculous character appears from the previous announcement of the plague, its intensity, the restriction of its victims to "the firstborn," and the complete exemption of the Israelites. It was a cruel infliction, yet it embodies an inevitable law of retribution. One cannot forget the command of that king who ordered the death of countless Hebrew children, nor the story of "bricks without straw," nor the groans of suffering slaves, the anguish of the brick kilns, the hiss of the taskmasters' cruel lash, the repeated warnings of the Lord, the broken promises, and the hard heart of Pharaoh.

Now, at last, the heart of the king is broken. He decrees the immediate dismissal of the Israelities from their pitiful bondage. He grants all the demands which have been made. There are no restrictions. So deeply has he been affected by the terrible calamity, that he abjectly begs a blessing from the men he has despised, rebuked, and driven from his presence under the threat of death: "And bless me also," he cries, imploring Moses to deliver him from any further calamity. The Egyptians shared the consternation of their king. They "gave" (not "lent") to the Israelites all they "asked" (not "borrowed"), "jewels of silver and jewels of gold and raiment." They were glad to be rid of these dangerous neighbors at any price. They neither expected nor wished them to return (Ch. 12:29-36).

THE DEPARTURE FROM EGYPT. [Ch. 12:37-51.]

The story of the actual exodus of Israel is told in a few lines. However, the brief narrative specifies the number of people and the length of time they had sojourned in Egypt. It further gives the reason for so naming the "Feast of Unleavened Bread," and it emphasizes the importance of the historic event to be commemorated by that annual festival.

The number of Israelites as given is "six hundred thousand . . . men." When to this are added the numbers of women and children, and also of the "mixed multitude" of "foreigners" that followed, the total is estimated at between two and three million persons. The problems involved in adapting these figures to the events of the forty years of wilderness wanderings are admittedly perplexing. These problems for the most part disappear if one accepts the suggestion made by the authors of the English Revised Version and of the American Revised Version. According to this suggestion the word "thousands" should be translated "families," or "clans." (See Numbers 1:16 margin.) Then the number of those who escaped from Egypt would be estimated at one hundred thousand souls. Even at this reckoning, it was a vast host to be organized and sustained on the long journeys across the deserts of Arabia.

The haste of their departure is indicated by the statement that "they baked unleavened cakes of dough which they brought forth out of Egypt, for it was not leavened; because they were thrust out of Egypt, and could not tarry, neither had they prepared for themselves any victual." Therefore, the Passover and the feast of seven days which followed have been celebrated through the centuries by the use of unleavened bread or "Passover bread." This custom has been carefully observed and has been regarded as an important feature of the ordinance established to call to mind the night in which the Israelites were set free from bondage, "a night to be observed unto the Lord for bringing them out from the land of Egypt." It was indeed a great deliverance, and it was a prophecy and a symbol of the redemption wrought by Christ. His followers are to "keep the feast," that is, they are to live their pure lives, "not with old leaven, neither with the leaven of malice and wickedness; but with the unleavened bread of sincerity and truth" (I Cor. 5:8).

The mention of the "mixed multitude" may ex-

plain the reason for the future directions as to the Passover which close the chapter (vss. 43 to 51). These
relate to the qualification of those who were permitted
to participate in the observance. They were required to
submit to the rite of circumcision as a sign that they
were to be identified with the covenant people of God.
On this condition, foreigners ("strangers"), and even
slaves, were admitted to the sacred feast.

In so far as the Lord's Supper has taken the place
of the Passover as a memorial of redemption a parallel
may be noted. Only those can rightfully partake of the
sacrament who belong to the body of believers, and it is
proper for such persons first to accept the rite of baptism, which is regarded as "a sign and seal of our in-
grafting into Christ." In a still deeper sense, only those
can truly benefit by participation in the sacrament who
in some real sense "discern" in the broken bread and
outpoured wine the Lord's body, and who trust Him as
their divine Redeemer. We are reminded further of the
truth that all who belong to Christ form one "people,"
one "brotherhood," so that rich and poor, bond and
free, citizen and foreigner, young and old, observe a real
"communion" and enjoy a true spiritual fellowship.

There is one phrase in this added instruction as
to the Passover (vss. 43-51) which brings us to Calvary
and the cross of Christ. It refers to the Paschal lamb
and states: "Neither shall ye break a bone thereof" (vs.
46). When the crucified Saviour was spared this last
indignity visited upon the dying robbers, John, the beloved disciple, who witnessed the scene, saw in the incident a fulfillment of this scripture (John 19:31-36).
This record emphasizes for us the truth presented in the

words of Paul: "Christ our passover is sacrificed for us" (I Cor. 5:7).

THE CONSECRATION OF THE FIRST-BORN [Ch. 13:1-16.]

We are saved to serve, and the condition of acceptable service is holiness of life. This is the message which every Christian should discern in the first recorded instructions given to the Children of Israel after their deliverance from Egypt. According to a divine requirement, all the first-born sons of the Israelites, and also all the first-born of the cattle were set aside as sacred to God. As He had spared the first-born of His people when the first-born of the Egyptians perished, it was reasonable that God should regard as His own those who owed their lives to His deliverance. The first-born of men were consecrated to holy service, the first-born of cattle were offered in sacrifice. The first-born of an animal which was not fit for a sacrifice was redeemed by offering a lamb. In later years, the tribe of Levi, in place of the first-born of the other tribes, was set aside to sacred ministry, but even then each eldest son was to be redeemed by the payment of five shekels of "ransom money." As on the night of the Passover, which this consecration of the first-born called to mind, salvation had come by the sacrifice of a lamb, so Christians believe that they have been "redeemed . . . with the precious blood of Christ, as of a lamb without blemish and without spot." Therefore, the redeemed are to regard themselves as belonging in reality to the Redeemer. Thus Paul insists: "Ye are not your own, for ye are bought with a price; therefore glorify God in your body, and in your spirit, which are God's" (I Cor. 6:19, 20).

This reference which Paul makes to redemption brings to mind the condition for service intimated in the ancient ritual. Paul is insisting upon holiness of life, and Moses united his instructions for the consecration of the first-born with a repetition of the institution of the Feast of Unleavened Bread. This feast was inseparable from the Feast of Passover. As leaven was a symbol of corruption, those who partook of the Passover must remove all leaven from their homes. So those who are redeemed by Christ belong to Christ, whose service requires the putting away of impurity and sin. They do not serve Him in order to be saved, but they serve Him, and seek to be like Him, because they have been saved. Redemption should be followed by consecration, and consecration demands purity and holiness of life. A redeemed people kept the Feast of Unleavened Bread and dedicated their first-born to the Lord.

There is a third important message contained in these instructions relative to the consecration of the first-born. It concerns the religious instruction of the young. The Israelites were to explain to their children the full meaning of their consecration and of the Feast of the Unleavened Bread. They were to explain the connection of these institutions with the great deliverance from Egypt which God had wrought. It is of vital importance today that Christians should teach their children the meaning of salvation and what is involved in redemption and consecration. Too rarely is this duty performed. In the case of the Israelites they were urged to keep the Passover and its meaning continually in their thoughts and in the minds of their households. The exhortation

was, "And it shall be for a sign unto thee upon thine
hand and for a memorial between thine eyes." This precept taken literally explains the practice among the Jews
of wearing phylacteries. These are small boxes contain-
ing strips of parchment on which are written extracts
from the Law. These phylacteries are fastened to the
left wrist and to the forehead at times of worship. Possibly, however, Moses was using a figure of speech, im-
plying the need of constant remembrance. In a very real
sense Christians have before them sacred symbols which
can be employed to teach the young the great truths of
redemption. These are the sacraments of baptism and
the Supper of our Lord. By these, or other signs and
symbols and means of instruction, the children of Christian parents should be made to understand and continually to remember the meaning of the salvation
wrought by Christ our Redeemer.

Divine Guidance. [Ch. 13:17-22.]

The redeemed of the Lord can depend upon the
guidance of the Lord. "It came to pass, when Pharaoh
had let the people go, that God led them." When one
has been delivered from the tyranny of selfishness and
sin and unbelief, he may expect to be divinely guided.
This direction of the journey is always gracious and
merciful, although at times perplexing and even discouraging. "God led them not through the way of the land
of the Philistines, although that was near; for God said,
Lest peradventure the people repent when they see war,
and they return to Egypt: But God led the people
about, through the way of the wilderness of the Red

Sea." The shortest route to Canaan, and apparently the easiest, was to the northeast along the coast of the Mediterranean Sea. The journey of the Israelites was deflected to the southeast through the peninsula of Sinai. The reason is clearly stated. The shorter route would have brought them at once into contact with the hostile and warlike Philistines. The Israelites were not prepared for battle, and they needed years of discipline before they were ready for the conquest of Canaan. So God guides us today. The journey may seem long and the trials may be great, but we have this blessed assurance: "God is faithful who will not suffer you to be tempted above that ye are able; but will with the temptation also make a way to escape, that ye may be able to bear it" (I Cor. 10:13).

The people were not ready for war. However, they "went up harnessed out of the land of Egypt," and this is sometimes understood to mean that they were "fully armed." Probably the words indicate that they were "marshalled" or "in orderly array." We are not to suppose that the Israelites fled from Egypt as a disorganized mob. Moses was too great a leader for that. Months of warning and preparation had preceded their departure. They had the benefit of discipline and went out in something like "military order." Wise organization should be sought by the people of God in every age.

The condition of guidance is faith. This is illustrated by the narrative: "And Moses took the bones of Joseph with him; for he had straitly sworn the children of Israel, saying, God will surely visit you; and ye shall carry up my bones away hence with you." The story of the bones of Joseph is a parable of faith. As the great prince and prime-minister was dying, he did not request that he should be buried in Egypt, the land in which he had lived in splendor and glory, but he gave a solemn charge to his brethren that he should be buried in the Land of Canaan. He believed that God would bring his people into that land. He looked across the intervening centuries to the fulfillment of the promises of God. So, many years after, as Moses starts on the long journey, he took with him "the bones of Joseph." That body, which had been embalmed and preserved, formed a strange but magnificent ensign as the people started on their march. It indicated an unfaltering belief that God would guard and keep them and bring them at last to the Land of Promise. So every Christian should go forward in a life of faith, believing that he is to be kept from falling and, in spite of weakness and failure, is to reach at last the land of heavenly rest.

"And they took their journey from Succoth," which probably was the headquarters of Israel, "and encamped in Etham," a frontier city in Egypt, "in the edge of the wilderness." That is the important point in a message of divine guidance. The wilderness is perplexing, not because there are no paths, but because there are so many that one who journeys needs some direction to know which path to choose.

"And the Lord went before them by day in a pillar of a cloud, to lead them the way; and by night in a pillar of fire, to give them light; to go by day and night." There was but one cloud. It was in the form of a pillar, which had the appearance of smoke by day and of fire by night. It was the symbol of the divine presence. It was a signal and a guide. When it moved, by day or night, the people moved. Where it stopped they encamped (Nums. 9:15-28).

Thus God guided His people of old. How does He guide us today? His word is an infallible rule of faith and practice. His Spirit speaks to us through His word. He has given us the faculty of conscience which always gives us the approval or disapproval of a moral choice. God expects us also to reason from the providences of life, to consult with friends, and, first of all, to turn to Him in prayer, submitting our wills to His. Whatever the instrument or the agency He may employ, we are to believe in the reality of His leading. The Shepherd Psalm sounds the inspiring note: "He leadeth me," and Paul assures us that "as many as are led by the Spirit of God they are the sons of God."

CROSSING THE SEA. [Ch. 14.]

Those who follow the guidance of God are not free from trials, temptations and peril; but the darkest night may prove to be the time when God most clearly reveals His grace and power. So it was with the Israelites when they were overtaken by Pharaoh, when the Lord opened for them a way of escape through the sea. Pharaoh "had let the people go," but he determined to pursue and capture them. His "heart was hardened," and this by a perfectly natural process. So often had he broken his word for fear the people might escape, that when they had left the land he was overcome with regret for the loss of this multitude of slaves. He could not help changing his mind once again. "The heart of Pharaoh and of his servants were turned against the people,

and they said, Why have we done this, that we have let
Israel go from serving us?" The armies of Egypt were
mustered in haste and were soon in hot pursuit, led by
the mad king. They overtook the fugitives "encamping
by the sea." The situation of the Israelites was desperate. They were shut in by mountains and desert and
sea, and now within sight were the chariots and horse-
men of Pharaoh.

Yet God had led them into this place of peril.
Had they continued their original course toward the
southeast their march would have been unobstructed,
but they had received a divine command to change the
direction and to turn due south. The result was their
present hopeless plight.

The guidance of God is beset by mystery. It
seems to have been His purpose to strengthen the faith
of His people by a great deliverance, and to overthrow
their cruel and confident enemy. Such indeed was the
issue. However, seeing their peril, "the children of Israel
cried out unto the Lord." It was a cry of terror. "They
were sore afraid." Then they turned on Moses with a
severe rebuke: Why had he brought them from Egypt?
It would have been better for them to remain slaves to
the Egyptians than to die in the wilderness.

The reply of Moses is one which the people of
God often need to remember: "Fear ye not, stand still,
and see the salvation of the Lord." Sometimes there is
nothing else for us to do but to stand still, to await the
deliverance which the Lord alone can give. On the
other hand, there are times for action, when prayer and
worship and faith alone are not sufficient. "And the
Lord said unto Moses, Wherefore criest thou unto me?

speak unto the children of Israel, that they go forward:
but lift thou up thy rod, and stretch out thine hand over
the sea, and divide it: and the children of Israel shall go
on dry ground through the midst of the sea." Then the
marvellous deliverance began. The pillar of fire moved
backward. "It came between the camp of the Egyptians
and the camp of Israel; and it was a cloud and darkness
to them, but it gave light by night to these. . . . And
Moses stretched out his hand over the sea; and the Lord
caused the sea to go back by a strong east wind all that
night, and made the sea dry land, and the waters were
divided. And the children of Israel went into the midst
of the sea upon the dry ground, and the waters were a
wall unto them on their right hand and on their left."

The Egyptians pursued the Israelites into the bed
of the sea, when suddenly they were blinded by an appalling light issuing from the dark cloud: "The Lord
looked unto the host of the Egyptians through the pillar of fire and of the cloud, and troubled the host of the
Egyptians." Some manifestation of the divine presence
threw the troops into consternation and panic. Then a
more terrible disaster developed. The chariot wheels
sank into the soft sand. Advance became more and
more difficult. The warriors concluded that supernatural forces were about to destroy them and cried: "Let
us flee from the face of Israel; for the Lord fighteth for
them." But through the confused mass of horses and
chariots flight became impossible. Then in the hour
of despair came the final catastrophe. Moses again
"stretched forth his hand over the sea . . . and the waters
returned, and covered the chariots, and the horse-
men, and all the host of Pharaoh; . . . there remained

not so much as one of them. But the children of Israel walked upon dry land in the midst of the sea. . . . Thus the Lord saved Israel that day out of the hand of the Egyptians."

Whatever natural means the Lord may have used in delivering His people, the forces of nature were His and employed by Him. However much the marvel may have been due to fierce winds, to flashes of lightning, to the ebb and flow of the tides, the event was miraculous; it was wrought by the direct power and intervention of God.

The Israelites had been encouraged by the words of Moses, and had come to rely upon the divine promise of deliverance. Their initial terror was transformed into sublime trust: "By faith they passed through the Red Sea as by dry land: which the Egyptians assaying to do were drowned." While believing that God acts through the powers of nature, we address our prayers to Him, we rest on His promises, we trust in His grace.

Paul uses this marvelous event in the history of Israel as both a warning and an encouragement to the followers of Christ: "Our fathers were under the cloud, and all passed through the sea, and were all baptized unto Moses in the cloud and in the sea." However, many of them proved untrue to Moses and fell into grievous sin. So we have been committed by baptism to be true to Christ our Leader. "Wherefore let him that thinketh he standeth take heed lest he fall." It is well for us to be warned. Also the encouragement is great as we think of the crossing of the Sea. "God is faithful who will . . . not suffer you to be tempted above that you are able, but will with the temptation also make a way to escape" (I Cor. 10:13). By every deliverance faith is strengthened. Thus the narrative concludes: "And Israel saw the great work which the Lord did upon the Egyptians: and the people feared the Lord, and believed the Lord, and his servant Moses" (Ch. 14:31).

THE SONG OF MOSES. [Ch. 15:1-21.]

The redeemed of the Lord love to praise their Redeemer, and in this praise the art of music finds its noblest use. Thus Miriam and the women of Israel, marking time with the stroke of timbrels and rhythmical movements, sang in response to the chorus of men the refrain of the magnificent hymn of triumph: "Sing ye to the Lord, for he hath triumphed gloriously; the horse and his rider hath he thrown into the sea."

This refrain repeats the note which opens the song composed to celebrate the deliverance of Israel from the hosts of Pharaoh. This noble hymn is no mere secular ode, no expression of pride, no mere exultation over a fallen foe. This is the *Te Deum* of Israel. It is a song of praise and gratitude to God. In it even the name of Moses is not mentioned. It was composed to recognize the goodness and power of the Lord who had interposed to secure the salvation of His people. As Passover was the Sign, this is the Song of Redemption.

It may be divided into two stanzas. The first points backward and describes the overthrow of the enemy (vss. 1-12); the second looks forward to the deliverances which were yet to come (vss. 13-18).

The destruction of the Egyptians is depicted with vivid touches, which indicate the impressions of an eye-witness. We see the proud array of the chariots and "chosen captains," and hear the cruel boasts of those who are pursuing the Israelites: "I will divide the spoil: my lust shall be satisfied upon them." Then we hear the roar of the wind, and see the waters standing "upright as an heap" and "congealed in the heart of the sea." Then the floods return, and the chariots, and charioteers encased in heavy armor, sink "into the bottom as a stone. . . . They sank as lead in the mighty waters." It is a picture of complete destruction and hopeless defeat (vss. 1-12).

Then come the promises of future triumphs. The enemies shall be overwhelmed with fear. "The inhabitants of Palestina, the dukes of Edom, the mighty men of Moab, . . . all the inhabitant of Canaan shall melt away." None shall stand before the advance of Israel. The redeemed people shall "pass over," they shall be brought into the Land of Promise, and planted in the place which the Lord has made for them to dwell in (vss. 13-18).

All this redemption, all these deliverances, all the future blessedness are attributed to the Lord. He is the strength and the "song" of His people. He is their "salvation." He has "triumphed gloriously." He "shall reign forever and forever."

Such is the Song of Redemption. Its notes have reached down the centuries. It is the first expression of the praise the people of God have repeated in countless hours when divine deliverance has been given to those in spiritual and in physical peril. Such in part is the anthem chanted by the redeemed in glory who stand by the sea of glass, "having the harps of God," and who "sing the song of Moses the servant of God and the song of the Lamb" (Rev. 15:2-3).

With this Song of Moses the first great division of the Book of Exodus reaches its climax and its close. The story which began with the descent into Egypt of Jacob and his sons reaches here a new chapter. The sons of Israel, long a race of slaves, have been delivered from bondage; they have left Egypt forever; they have entered another continent of the globe; they have begun a new life. They have sung their song of deliverance. Their faces are now set toward a new land as the redeemed people of God.

II

THE JOURNEY TO SINAI EXODUS 15:22 to 18:27

BITTER WATERS MADE SWEET. [Ch. 15:22-26.]

CHRISTIANS always have found instruction and inspiration from comparisons drawn between the wilderness experiences of Israel and those on "the journey of life." In the case of Israel the first of these experiences was one of disillusion and disappointment. It came to them at Marah. Indeed, the three days' journey from the Red Sea to Marah had been in itself a disillusion. Delivered by a miracle from their Egyptian enemies and assured that all their foes were to melt away before them, they sang their song of praise and started forward in high hopes; but the way was hard and discouraging. It led them over rocks and burning sands. No trees or vegetation were in sight. They thirsted for water. Then in the distance appeared signs of life. They drew near to gleaming pools. Rejoicing, they stooped to drink, when, lo, the water was bitter. The place was called Marah, which means "bitterness." It was a veritable symbol of disappointment. "Walking through the wilderness of this world," the children of God frequently look with passionate longing upon some goal which when reached proves to be utterly distressing, unsatisfying, mere "vanity and vexation of spirit." That which promised to fill the heart with joy is found to bring only sorrow and pain.

"And the people murmured against Moses, saying, What shall we drink? And he cried unto the Lord; and the Lord shewed him a tree, which when he had cast into the waters, the waters were made sweet." A natural object was used. A natural process was involved. Yet it was under divine direction and attended by supernatural power. So God deals with His children today. He is ever healing waters which are bitter. He employs some providence, some unexpected event, some friendship, some surprising success, some new view of life, some message from His word, some deeper knowledge of Christ, and the keenest disappointment becomes a source of delight. The ancient writers were right, indeed, in calling to mind one "Tree," and in declaring that the cross of Christ is sweetening all the bitter waters of the world.

From this experience at Marah God took occasion to draw a lesson. He promised the people that, as He had healed the water, so, if they would do that which was "right in his sight," and "give ear to His commandments," He would heal them and protect them from diseases of the body and by implication from diseases of the spirit. God does give real relief from disappointment and distress of mind, and each new experience turns us to Him with stronger faith that He can deliver us from even greater sorrows and can give healing to our souls (Ch. 15:22-26).

SEASONS OF REFRESHING. [Ch. 15:27.]

It was not far from Marah to Elim. The place where disillusion has been divinely dispelled is often near to a scene of refreshment and new life. The journey from the Red Sea to Marah was through thirty-three miles of dreary desert. It was only six miles from Marah to Elim. "The sweetness and bitterness of life lie very near each other after all." "They came to Elim, where were twelve wells of water, and threescore and ten palm trees: and they encamped there by the waters." It was a rich and verdant oasis. There they rested. From this place of delight they started with new courage on their journey toward Sinai. The Christian life is not wholly a desert journey. It often leads through "green pastures and beside still waters." There are many refreshing experiences which enable us to renew our journey toward the rising sun, toward the mountain of God (Ch. 15:27).

BREAD FROM HEAVEN. [Ch. 16.]

The most important incident on the wilderness journey was the gift of *manna*. This was a miraculous supply of food which was continued all through the years, until the children of Israel reached the land of Canaan. The people had other forms of nourishment. For example, the story here mentions a supply of quail at the very time manna was first given. The indication is that manna was supplied daily, whenever needed, through the wilderness journey. It was described as "a small round thing, as small as the hoar frost on the ground. . . . It was like coriander seed, white; and the taste of it was like wafers made with honey." There are natural products somewhat corresponding to this description. The manna of the peninsula of Sinai, for instance, is a sweet juice which in warm weather exudes from the trunk and branches of the tamarisk and forms small round white grains, which rapidly melt in the heat; its taste is sweet, and it is often compared to honey. The food supplied to the Israelites was so similar in character that they naturally called it manna. However, this bread which was "rained from heaven" was evidently supernatural, both because of its quantity and its qualities. It was given in such abundance as to supply a vast multitude with food at all seasons and during a long period of years. It could be gathered daily for six days, but on the seventh day none appeared. On the sixth day twice the usual amount could be secured, and half could be kept for the seventh day. That gathered any other day became corrupt and useless if kept overnight.

The first obvious message is that of the gracious provision which God makes for His people. This provision was intended to teach them dependence, and obedience. He gives them food enough for each day. They may expect enough for gratitude, but not enough for greed. They must labor to secure the needed supply, even as they pray, "Give us this day our daily bread."

A second clear message is the divine provision of a seventh day of rest. Even before the Commandments expressed this law it is here clearly stated as an absolute rule of human life and well-being. Six days of labor should be followed by a day of holy, joyous rest and refreshment.

The spiritual interpretation of this gracious gift

of manna finds in it a type of Christ. This is in accordance with the teaching of our Lord Himself. When in a desert place He had fed five thousand men with a few "loaves and fishes," He interpreted the miracle in the terms of this Old Testament story. He was Himself the true bread which came down from heaven. He said: "I am the bread of life; he that cometh to me shall never hunger, and he that believeth on me shall never thirst" (John 6:35). To those who truly appropriate Him in real faith and identify themselves with Him, He gives life in all its richness and fulness. It is even a symbol of the joys of heaven: "To him that overcometh will I give to eat of the hidden manna." To commemorate the goodness of God, it was decreed that a pot of manna should be preserved for the instruction of future generations. This was placed in the Holy of Holies of the Tabernacle. In such a provision it is not difficult to trace a comparison with the memorial observance in the Supper of our Lord, when by faith we partake of Him, the Bread of Life (Ch. 16:1-36).

THE RIVEN ROCK. [Ch. 17:1-7.]

Christ is the Bread of Life (John 6:35); He also gives Living Water (John 4:10). Paul found both of these truths illustrated in the wilderness journey of Israel, the first in the gift of manna, the second in the experience at Rephidim. Here the people were in dire distress. Their previous sufferings had been severe but not desperate; now their anguish is intolerable. They have been passing for days through a burning desert, and amid its glare and heat all supplies of water have failed.

The pools at Marah had been bitter, now there is no water at all. The name "Rephidim" means "resting-places," and usually the oasis is clad in verdure and supplied with abundant streams. Now all is scorched and barren, the pools and wells are dry. The expectations of the people are bitterly disappointed. By their deadly thirst they are driven to a frenzy. They "murmured against Moses, and said, Wherefore is this that thou has brought us up out of Egypt, to kill us and our children and our cattle with thirst?" They had "murmured" before—at the Red Sea when overtaken by Pharaoh, at Marah because of the bitter waters, in the wilderness before manna was given them; but this murmuring was far more serious and unrestrained. It was accompanied even by threats of violence. "What shall I do unto this people?" Moses cried unto the Lord, "they be almost ready to stone me." Such murmuring was faithless and ignoble; yet we must not forget the horror of their thirst, nor how natural it is to prefer bondage in Egypt to death in the desert.

"And the Lord said unto Moses, Go on before the people, and take with thee of the elders of Israel; and thy rod, wherewith thou smotest the river, take in thine hand, and go. Behold, I will stand before thee there upon the rock in Horeb; and thou shalt smite the rock, and there shall come water out of it, that the people may drink. And Moses did so in the sight of the elders of Israel."

With this memorable scene in mind Paul boldly declares: "And that rock was Christ." He means that it was a symbol of Christ. Then, since the miracle was repeated on the wilderness journey, he refers to the "Rock that followed them." He indicates that as repeatedly water was given to the people by divine power, so through all his pilgrimage the Christian finds in Christ a source of refreshment, a fountain of life.

So it is that the apostle interprets the gift of manna and the riven rock as types of Christ, and declares of Israel, as his words are quoted more fully, "They did all eat the same spiritual meat; and did all drink the same spiritual drink, for they drank of that spiritual Rock that followed them; and that Rock was Christ" (I Cor. 10:3-4). As we partake of this spiritual, typical, sacramental food and drink, we should remember that the words of the apostle are part of a serious warning. So the names by which Rephidim was to be remembered, "Massah and Medibah," called to mind not so much the deliverance wrought by God as the failure and murmuring of the people. Even those who partake of the divinely provided food and drink are subject to severe temptation. Specifically, they are tempted to murmur. "Neither murmur ye," writes the apostle, "as some of them murmured." Partakers of Christ, we are to depend upon Him for deliverance from peril, and to learn in whatsoever state we are "therewith to be content," believing that "God will supply" our "need, according to his riches in glory by Christ Jesus."

CONFLICT AND VICTORY. [Ch. 17:8-16.]

Those who have been baptized into Christ, who have been sustained by spiritual food and drink, and have found "resting-places" as had Israel at Rephidim, are not free from assault and conflict (Eph. 6:12), but they can be assured of victory if they follow Joshua ("Jesus") and fight under the banner of the Lord. Such seems to be the symbolic message contained in the story of the attack and the defeat of the Amalekites. This fierce and warlike people were the most powerful of those nomadic tribes which wandered over the peninsula of Sinai. They looked with apprehension and resentment on the hordes of Israelites which had swarmed into their country. They determined to destroy the intruders. Attacking them in the rear, when Israel was on the march, they cut off many of the stragglers, "the feeble and faint and weary" (Deut. 25:17-19), and encamped ready to inflict a more serious blow on the morrow. Then Moses planned his strange strategy of battle. He put Joshua in command of the armed forces. With the rod of God in his hand, he ascended a hill, accompanied by Aaron and Hur. "And Moses, Aaron and Hur went up to the top of the hill. And it came to pass, when Moses held up his hand, that Israel prevailed: and when he let down his hand, Amalek prevailed. But Moses' hands were heavy; and they took up a stone and put it under him, and he sat thereon; and Aaron and Hur stayed up his hands, the one on the one side, the other on the other side; and his hands were steady until the going down of the sun. And Joshua discomfited Amalek and his people with the edge of the sword."

This picture of Moses on the hill with uplifted hands has been taken properly as a symbol of intercession. No doubt Moses was lifting up his heart in prayer. As he became exhausted, he needed the support of his two companions. They gave him strength and encouragement to continue his supplications, and they observed that the fluctuations of the battle coincided with the position of Moses' hands. The answer to his petition was a notable victory over the enemy.

It should be observed, however, that while Moses and his companions prayed on the hilltop, Joshua and his troops fought valiantly on the plain, for prayer to God must be accompanied by faithful human effort. In this scene of Moses praying for the hosts of Israel has been found a symbol also of the Saviour interceding on high for His people as they struggle here below.

The supreme message of the story is interpreted by Moses himself. He received a divine assurance of the final destruction of the cruel enemy, and he "built an altar and called the name of it Jehovah-nissi" ("the Lord is my banner"). The altar was not only for sacrifice or worship but a memorial of a great victory which was wrought, as the name declared, by the power of God. It is a testimony to that fact that one who fights in the name of the Lord, with trust in Him, and for His cause, is certain to triumph. Under the banner of the Lord victory is assured.

WISE COUNSEL. [Ch. 18:1-27.]

A belief in divine guidance should not make one indifferent to the advice of friends. Indeed, kindly counsel from those we trust is an instrument God frequently employs to direct our way. This is possibly the message embodied in the story of the visit of Jethro to Moses. The great leader of Israel was following faithfully the pillar of cloud and of fire; but his health was preserved and his usefulness increased by his humbly accepting the sympathetic suggestion of a near relative.

Jethro was the "father-in-law," or probably the brother-in-law, of Moses. With him Moses had lived for many years previous to his call to deliver Israel. As he left to assume his difficult and perilous task, he sent back his wife and children to be under the care of Jethro. Now deliverance has been achieved. Word reaches Jethro that Moses has brought the people, by divine help, out of the land of bondage, across the desert, to the foot of Mount Sinai. Taking with him Zipporah and her two sons, he arranges a meeting with Moses as Israel is encamped near the mountain. The story is one of real charm. In contrast with all the previous scenes of the exodus, with its tragedy and suffering, here is a picture of personal affection, of sympathy and love. Jethro, as a priest, offers sacrifices of thanksgiving to God, and then, with the family circle and the leaders of Israel, partakes of the sacrificial feast.

The day following, Jethro observes how Moses is burdened and overwhelmed by his official duties, serving from morning to night as the sole judge of the people. He asks why Moses assumes such a task alone. The reply is that the people regard Moses' decisions as having divine sanction, and, further, that he employs his opportunity to instruct the people in the laws of God. Then "Moses' father-in-law said unto him, The thing that thou doest is not good. Thou wilt surely wear away, both thou, and this people that is with thee: for this thing is too heavy for thee; thou art not able to perform it thyself alone." That is to say, the strength of Moses will be overtaxed and the patience of the people will be exhausted as they wait for justice in such an overcrowded court.

Therefore, Moses is advised to continue to present serious cases to God in prayer, and to teach the people "ordinances" and "laws," "the way in which they must walk," and "the work" that each must do. However, he is to appoint "out of all the people . . . rulers of thousands, and rulers of hundreds, rulers of fifties and rulers of tens: and let them judge the people at all seasons, and it shall be, that every great matter they shall bring unto thee, but every small matter they shall judge: so shall it be easier for thyself, and they shall bear the burden with thee. . . . Then thou shalt be able to endure, and all this people shall also go to their place in peace."

It should be noted that this advice made the wise distinction between enacting laws and administering justice. It should also be observed how careful were the qualifications of judges as prescribed by Jethro; they were to be "able men," that is, fitted to exercise the office of judges, God-fearing, truthful, and "hating covetousness." The first of these qualifications assumes the other two, the last is peculiarly necessary in courts of justice.

As Jethro leaves for his home, one realizes the greatness of the service he has rendered by the prudent counsel he has offered to his relative, and as "Moses hearkened unto the voice of his father-in-law and did all that he had said," he shows himself to be an able administrator. First, he was willing to accept unselfish advice. Second, he adopted the principle of distributing responsibility, illustrating the homely adage that "it is better to set ten men to work than to attempt the work of ten men." In the third place, as recorded later (Deut. 1:13), he left to the people the privilege of selecting their own rulers and judges.

The modern reader may feel that he lives in days when religious work is overorganized; but this important incident points to the peril of the other extreme, and intimates the absolute necessity of order and system and co-operation in Christian life and service.

III

THE LAW EXODUS 19 to 24

The Covenant with Jehovah. [Ch. 19.]

FROM Egypt to Sinai was a distance of one hundred and fifty miles. Marching slowly, and with long halts at various places on their journey, the Israelites required two full months to reach the sacred mountain. Eleven months were spent there (Numbers 10:11, 12), and there, at the foot of Sinai, Israel was organized formally as a nation. There they made a covenant with God. They engaged to keep His commandments and He promised to be their king. The government thus constituted has been calleed a "theocracy," or "rule of God." He was to be the head of the nation, and in Him all the powers of the state, legislative, executive, and judicial, were to be united. Moses was to be His accredited representative, through whom He would exercise His rule.

The giving of the fundamental law which the people were to obey and the solemn ratification of the covenant are recorded in Exodus 19 to 24. The central chapters (20 to 23) contain the legal code. The last (Ch. 24) describes the solemn ceremony by which the covenant, based upon the keeping of these laws, was ratified. Chapter 19 records the formation of the covenant and depicts the impressive circumstances under which the law was given and the covenant was made.

In stating His requirement of obedience and loyalty, God reminds the people of his grace and care. He employs a beautiful if familiar image: "Ye have seen what I did unto the Egyptians, and how I bare you on eagles' wings, and brought you unto myself." For it is said that when the fledglings begin to fly, the eagle hovers round them and beneath them, ready to give needed support on its expanded wings.

Then is voiced the gracious *promise:* "Now therefore, if *ye will obey my voice* indeed, and keep my covenant, *then ye shall be* a peculiar treasure unto me above all people [or "from among all peoples"]: for all the earth is mine: and ye shall be unto me a kingdom of priests, and an holy nation." These words are applied by Peter to the Christian Church (I Peter 2:9). A "chosen generation" or an "elect race": this phrase, employed by Peter, is implied in the Old Testament narrative (so Isa. 43:20). "A peculiar treasure" denotes a personal possession, acquired at great cost, and carefully guarded. The phrase is translated beautifully, if incorrectly, as "my jewels" (Mal. 3:17). "A kingdom of priests": Israel collectively was to be a royal and a priestly race, representing God, its king, to all the world. "An holy nation": this holiness was to consist in a special consecration to God, and accordingly in purity and freedom from all pollution.

This condition of obedience Israel readily accepts: "And all the people answered together, and said, All that the Lord hath spoken we will do." Yet they never did. In view of the great privileges offered, they were willing to promise implicit obedience to the laws of God. Little did they realize the strictness of those laws or the weakness of human nature. In later years they seemed to forget that the covenant with God bound them to obedience. They seemed to imagine that the promised blessings were unconditional and that they could presume upon their position as the chosen people of God. From this false security they were never fully aroused (Jer. 7:4-16; Matt. 3:9; 8:11, 12; 21:31).

As all that God had done for Israel had not been deserved, so all that He was to do and to be would be granted in grace. It could not be earned. It might be lost by disobedience. God is not only gracious, He is just and righteous and ready to punish the disregard and transgression of His laws. This holiness of God and the sanctity of His commandments are illustrated by the dread and terrifying circumstances under which the law was committed to Moses. For the purpose of this divine communication God promised to come down upon the mountain; but He first commanded the people to purify themselves, and gave a solemn warning that no one should touch the mountain onto which He was to descend. "And it came to pass on the third day in the morning, that there were thunders and lightnings, and a thick cloud upon the mount, and the voice of the trumpet exceeding loud; so that all the people that was in the camp trembled. And Moses brought forth the people out of the camp to meet with God; and they stood at the nether part of the mount. And mount Sinai was altogether on a smoke, because the Lord descended upon it in fire: and the smoke thereof ascended as the smoke of a furnace, and the whole mount quaked greatly. And when the voice of the trumpet sounded long, and waxed louder and louder, Moses spake, and

God answered him by a voice. And the Lord came down upon Mount Sinai, on the top of the mount: and the Lord called Moses up to the top of the mount; and Moses went up" (Ch. 19:16-20).

In the Epistle to the Hebrews this whole scene is reproduced to show the contrast between the experience of Israel when making the Old Covenant and the privileges of Christians under the New. All efforts to save ourselves by keeping the law bring us to the terrors of Sinai; but by faith in Christ we become citizens of the heavenly Jerusalem, angels are our servants, we hold fellowship with a body of first-born ones, and stand in a new relation to God and to those whose consciences have been cleansed by the sanctifying, redeeming blood of Christ, by which the New Covenant has been sealed (Heb. 12:22-24).

However, great privileges imply grave responsibility. If Israel, at Sinai, dared not to disobey God as He spoke through Moses, how much less can we refuse to obey Him as He speaks to us through Christ. If Israel did not venture to touch the mountain on which God was revealed, how much less dare we draw near to God, trusting in our own merits and refusing the saving work of our divinely appointed Mediator. With abiding faith in Him "let us have grace whereby we may serve God acceptably with reverence and godly fear, for our God is a consuming fire" (Heb. 12:25-28).

THE TEN COMMANDMENTS. [Ch. 20:1-17.]

The Decalogue, or the "Ten Words," or the "Ten Commandments," also is called the "Testimony"

(Ch. 25:16) and the "Covenant" (Ch. 34:28). It constituted the fundamental law of the nation; it was, in fact, the Constitution of the Twelve United Tribes of Israel; it was the essential basis of the Covenant with Jehovah. Its supreme importance was indicated in that its Ten Words were spoken "to the Assembly of Israel" by God Himself out of the "thick darkness with a great voice" (Deut. 5:22). How the sound was produced it is idle to conjecture. God is a spirit and He is really present in the agents which perform His will. Thus, in the New Testament, the law is said to have been given through the ministration of angels (Acts 7:53; Gal. 3:19; Heb. 2:2). However, the "great voice" was terrifying to the people and gave divine sanction to the words which were uttered.

The importance of this Law is further emphasized by the statement that the Ten Words were graven by the finger of God on two tables of stone (Ch. 31:18) to assure their permanent record. These tables were placed in the innermost shrine of the tabernacle where God manifested His glory and received the worship of His people.

While thus the commandments were of such supreme importance to Israel, they are of equal significance for all nations. They are a matchless summary of all the duties which God requires of man; they furnish a perfect standard of moral conduct, they express the abiding principles of right living, and set forth the true relation of man to man and of man to God.

These moral principles did not originate with Moses. They belong to the very constitution of human life and society. Long before the Ten Words were written on tables of stone, murder and adultery and lying and theft were recognised as wrong; but it is the glory of Moses and of Israel that through them these eternal principles of right were given to the world in their matchless form.

Christ did not amend or abrogate or alter the Ten Commandments. He regarded them as perfect and changeless (Matt. 5:20), but He saw the need of rescuing them from the misconceptions and false additions of the Pharisees. He gave them their true spiritual interpretation. He taught that from the beginning they applied to thought and motive as well as to act and deed. He insisted that their transgression would be not merely an injury to man but a sin against God. The followers of Christ are free from the obligations of the ceremonial law, but more than ever are bound by the moral law, not as a means of salvation, but as a rule of life. They keep the commandments not to win the favor of Christ, but in gratitude for His redeeming grace, not in their own strength, but by the power of His spirit.

Christ did not even give an original summary of the commandments, as many seem to suppose. The words, "Thou shalt love the Lord thy God with all thine heart, and with all thy soul, and with all thy might" and "thou shalt love thy neighbor as thyself" were the words of Moses (Deut. 6:5; Levit. 19:18). They were understood by all students of the Law in the day of Christ to be a complete and familiar summary of the Law (Luke 10:25-28). It was no new discovery that all the commandments are fulfilled in obedience to the law of love. What Christ did do was to give a new standard of love, "that a man should lay down his life for his friends"; He gave a supreme example, "as I have loved you"; He gave a new motive, namely, His love for us: "The love of Christ constraineth us"; He "loved me and gave Himself for me."

Above all, Christ gave to those who trust and obey Him power to keep the commandments. "For what the law could not do in that it was weak through the flesh, God sending his own Son in the likeness of sinful flesh and for sin, condemned sin in the flesh that the righteous demands of the law might be fulfilled in us who walk not after the flesh, but after the Spirit" (Rom. 8:3, 4).

As to the numbering and divisions of the commandments there is some difference of view. The common enumeration followed by the Protestant and Greek churches is that of Philo and Josephus. The Jews regard the "Preface" as the "First Word" and unite the First and Second Commandments as the "Second Word." The Roman and Lutheran churches combine the First and Second Commandments and divide the Tenth into two, to complete the number.

So, too, while there is no doubt that the "Ten Words" were divided into two tables, some assign four to the first table and six to the second; while others assign five to each table. In this case the first table deals with the duties owed to God, and the second with those due to man. The symmetrical arrangement of five commandments to each table, while less common, has the support of many authorities, both ancient and modern. In its favor the claim is made that filial piety was formerly regarded as a religious rather than a moral obligation, and that, in Romans 13:9, where the complete Second Table appears to be spoken of, no mention is made of the Fifth Commandment. In either case there is a deep significance in the order of the "two tables." Duty to God precedes duty to man; duty to God is more difficult to fulfil than duty to man; duty to God results in the performance of duty to man. When Christ wished to show the lawyer his failure to keep the law, He mentioned only one's love to one's neighbor (Luke 10:25-37). So when He wished to test the "rich young ruler," He demonstrated only the young ruler's failure to love his neighbor as himself. Religion is the only firm basis for morality. The first and supreme need of the world is love for God. Love for man is sure to follow. Men who perform their duties to God, and love Him with the whole heart, are sure to fulfil their duties to their fellow men (Matt. 22:15-22).

The Preface to the Commandments is found in these words: "I am the Lord thy God, which have brought thee out of the land of Egypt, out of the house of bondage." This bases all moral obligation on the revealed will of God. The decalogue rests on divine authority; from its demands there can be no appeal.

However, the motive which impels to the willing performance of every duty is gratitude to God for His redeeming love. As in the case of Israel, His favor is unmerited, and it has resulted in a great deliverance. "We love because he first loved us" (Titus 2:11-14; 3:4-7; I John 4:19, R.V.).

The *First Commandment*, "Thou shalt have no other gods before me," or "beside me," meant that no other gods should be worshipped in addition to Jehovah.

The Israelites were not tempted to substitute other gods in His place, but rather to share with false gods their allegiance to Him. Thus Christians are not inclined to give up their faith in God so much as they are to adopt other objects with which they divide the devotion due to God alone. "Him only shalt thou serve" (Matt. 4:10).

The *Second Commandment*. "Thou shalt not make unto thee any graven image. . . . Thou shalt not bow down thyself to them nor serve them," had no reference to works of art, to painting or sculpture, but forbad the worship of God under the form of physical images. The heart of God is pained when the honor due Him is given to objects created by the hand of man, when "his glory is given to another" (Isa. 42:8). By an inevitable law, such idolatry results in immorality, and the penalty passes on to future generations. However, the consequences of sin, not its guilt, are transmitted; they often can be overcome, and the inheritance of virtue is quite as real. Furthermore, the just judgments of God are far surpassed by the "mercy" He shows "to them that love" Him.

The *Third Commandment*, "Thou shalt not take the name of the Lord thy God in vain," is not merely a prohibition of profanity. It is that, and as such is distressingly disregarded in the present day. More specifically, however, the commandment forbids perjury (Lev. 19:12). It indicates the sacredness of an oath. Yet the "name of the Lord" denotes not merely a title, but includes all that by which He makes Himself known and all that He shows himself to be. If we claim the Lord as our God we are hereby warned against bringing disrepute upon Him by any impure word or deed or by any insincere profession. Punishment will surely overtake the offender. "The Lord will not hold him guiltless that taketh His name in vain."

The *Fourth Commandment*, "Remember the Sabbath day, to keep it holy," is the formal enactment of a law previously recognized in connection with the gathering of manna (Ex. 16). Here it is stated to be in conformity with God's own creative work, which intimated a proper proportion of time between rest and labor. It taught men to regard work, not as an incessant, wearisome round, but as looking forward to fruition and enjoyment and rest. The Sabbath was regarded as of such supreme importance in expressing faith and obedience on the part of God's people that it was called a "sign of the covenant" between Israel and Jehovah (Ex. 31:13, 17; Ezekiel 20:12, 20). Our Lord did not abrogate this law, but showed how it should be kept, in rest and worship and deeds of mercy. His great claim as "Lord of the sabbath" was not that of controlling an outworn tradition, but of an abiding and most sacred institution (Mark 2:23 to 3:6). The change from the seventh to the first day of the week was made to commemorate the resurrection of Christ and indicates that we stand not on the ground of creation, but on redemption ground. The Sabbath is prophetic of "the rest" which yet remains "for the people of God" (Heb. 4:9).

Thus the First Commandment declares the unity of God as opposed to all systems of polytheism. The second emphasizes the spirituality of God and condemns all idolatry. The third implies His holiness and the supreme claim He has on the reverence of man. The fourth recognizes that all time, all labor and rest, are to be consecrated to God.

The *Fifth Commandment*, "Honour thy father and thy mother," is recognized by Christ as of abiding obligation by His severe rebuke of the Pharisees for their disregard of this law and by His touching example of making loving provision for His mother even in the hour of His agony (John 19:25-27). By his statement that it is "the first commandment with promise," Paul reminds Christian children of the particular importance to them of this commandment. The exact meaning of this promise "that thy days may be long upon the land which the Lord thy God giveth thee" is open to question; but the use made by Paul in applying the promise to the children of Christians would indicate that the application is individual rather than national.

The *Sixth Commandment*, "Thou shalt not kill," and the *Seventh Commandment*, "Thou shalt not commit adultery," were not abrogated or supplemented by our Lord. He stripped them of the false limitations handed down by "those of old time," and gave to them their true interpretation and the meaning which had been theirs from the beginning. He insisted that they applied not only to outward acts but to inner thoughts and motives. A sinful desire is not so great a fault as a sinful deed, but it is as truly a breach of the law. The Sixth Commandment declared the sacredness of human life; the Seventh Commandment defended the sanctity of family ties.

The *Eighth Commandment*, "Thou shalt not steal," definitely defends the right of private property and declares that this must be respected quite as much as the person and the domestic peace of our neighbor. Framers of Utopias have advocated communism and imagined a social order in which private property would not exist. Such denial of a natural right does not have the sanction of Scripture. Our Saviour taught the principle of stewardship, namely, that all wealth is a sacred trust, for the use of which we some day must render an account to Him. The Early Church, only for a time and only in Jerusalem, practiced a form of "community of goods"; but this was local, occasional, temporary, and voluntary; those who wished retained their lands and houses (Acts 2:44, 45; 5:1-11). There are many ways of breaking the Eighth Commandment: unjust wages, unfaithful service, dishonest gains, cruelty, oppression, destruction of employer's property; these and other forms of theft endanger the social order.

The *Ninth Commandment*, "Thou shalt not bear false witness against thy neighbor," safeguards reputation, even as the Eighth Commandment protects private property; in fact, calumny may injure one more than robbery. "False witness" is most evil when it takes the form of perjury in a court of justice, but it also includes slander, hypocrisy, flattery, exaggeration and the imputing to others of false motives. It is startling but instructive to trace through the Bible what is said of lying and of liars; for example, Genesis 3:4; 12:10-20; 27:1-45; 37:25-35; I Samuel 22:7-23; II Kings 5:20-27; Acts 5:1-11; Revelation 21:8; 22:15.

The *Tenth Commandment*, "Thou shalt not covet," condemns the sin that lies at the heart of many modern socialistic movements, as it forbids every desire to secure for oneself that which belongs rightfully to another. It is the most searching of all the commandments. It belongs not merely to the realm of deed, but applies to thought and motive. It indicates that the Decalogue is more than a code of civil laws, it is spiritual in its very essence. This is illustrated by the experience of Paul. He felt himself blameless in the sight of the law until he judged himself by this precept. It was the means of revealing to him the holiness of the law. It brought him to despair until he found liberty through faith in Christ (Rom. 7:7-8:4).

Every serious review of the *Ten Commandments* turns one eagerly forward from Sinai to Calvary, to an empty tomb, to a risen Saviour, a Redeemer, a living Lord.

THE SECONDARY LAWS. [Ch. 20:18 to 23:33.]

Following the Ten Commandments, and based upon their principles, a series of laws is recorded which is known as *"The Book of the Covenant."* At the request of the people, who had been so terrified by the "voice of God," these laws were communicated to Moses and by Moses to the people (Ex. 20:18-21). They related to worship, to human rights, to personal conduct, and to sacred seasons and sacrifice.

The laws concerning worship (Ch. 20:23-26) provide that it should be offered with reverence, with simplicity, with propriety. There should be places of worship, altars of earth or unhewn stone. The worship should be accompanied by sacrifice, which is the symbol of dedication to God. There should be no such accompaniments as to indicate or lead to idolatry. At such places of true worship, God promised to Israel, as He promises to His people today, "I will come unto thee and I will bless thee" (Ch. 20:22-26).

The Laws concerning the Rights of Persons begin with that class most in need of protection and sympathy, namely, slaves. The Mosaic Law did not abolish slavery. It did regulate and ameliorate the institution. It recognized the right of a slave to just and humane treatment. The Hebrew master was to treat his slave less like a chattel than like a brother or a hired servant. Man-stealing, the basis of most modern slavery, was punished by death. A slave was bound for six years, at the most, and then set free. He could hold property and redeem himself. He was protected from violence, and must be compensated for bodily injury. His position has been likened to "a comparatively mild apprenticeship." In the day of Moses the time for the abolition of slavery had not arrived. Christ and· His apostles did not attempt to resort to violence to overthrow this or other social institutions; they taught brotherhood, humanity, and charity which made slavery and other social abuses impossible (Ch. 21:1-11).

Three Offences Punishable by Death are included in the Mosaic code: murder, kidnapping, and smiting or cursing father or mother. Cities of refuge were provided for cases of unintentional homicide (Ch. 21:12-17).

Laws of Compensation for Injury to Life and Limb are added. Here appears the provision of "an eye for an eye, and a tooth for a tooth." This was a right principle to guide the administration of justice. It did not need to be taken literally, but it did mean that "the penalty should fit the crime." What our Saviour forbad was taking a regulation designed for a court of law and using it as an excuse for personal revenge and individual retaliation (Matt. 6:38-42). As an injury might be caused by an animal as well as by a man, regulations were added which considered how far the owner of the animal was responsible, and what penalty should be exacted (Ch. 21:18-32).

Laws concerning the Rights of Property follow naturally, as an injury caused by an animal at once raises the question as to an injury caused to an animal. For such and similar cases of injury to property laws of compensation are provided (Ch. 21:33-36).

For *theft* the penalty was a double, in some cases even a fourfold, restoration. Laws are added for the punishment of trespassing upon property, and also for abusing the duties of trusteeship (Ch. 22:1-15).

The remaining portions of The Book of the Covenant are comprised of *Miscellaneous Laws* so diverse in character as to defy any exact analysis or classification. These include penalties for seduction, for witchcraft, and for the oppression of foreigners, of widows and orphans (Ch. 22:16-24). Usury is forbidden, and the payment to God of the *firstfruits* is required (Ch. 22:25-31).

Four commands follow. They are addressed to the conscience, with no mention of specific penalties. They forbid circulating a false report, supporting others who are bearing false witness, joining with a majority in an unjust judgment, or perverting justice in favor of the poor (Ch. 23:1-3). Active kindness even to an enemy is enjoined (Ch. 23:4, 5). Judges are warned to do justice to the poor, to be cautious in inflicting capital punishment in doubtful cases, to accept no bribes, and to vindicate the rights of foreigners (Ch. 23:6-9). The sabbatical year is recognized, and the observance enjoined of the three great annual festivals, namely, "The Feast of Unleavened Bread" (and Passover), "The Feast of Harvest" (Pentecost), and the "Feast of Ingathering" (Tabernacles). They were all feasts of thanksgiving, and in celebrating them offerings were to be brought in recognition of the goodness of the Lord (Ch. 23:10-19).

The Book of the Covenant closes with promises of the continual presence and guidance of God, of help in overcoming enemies, of material prosperity, and of widening dominion; but these promises are accompanied by solemn exhortations and threatenings; the people are to serve Jehovah alone and are to make no covenants with the heathen nations or their gods (Ch. 23:20-33).

SEALING THE COVENANT. [Ch. 24:1-11.]

The narrative of 20:21 is here resumed (vss. 1, 2): "And Moses came and told the people all the words of the Lord," that is, after he had received these words on the mountain. When he had told "the people all the words and commandments, all the people answered with one accord, All the words which the Lord hath said will we do" (vs. 3 continues 23:33). These words "Moses wrote," and they constitute *"the Book of the Covenant."* The next morning Moses arranges the ceremony for the solemn sealing of the covenant. He "builded an altar" to symbolize the presence of God, who was one party to the covenant, "and twelve pillars" to symbolize the presence of the Twelve Tribes, the other party. "Burnt offerings" and "peace offerings" were sacrificed, the former to indicate gratitude and the dedication of the people to the service of God, and the latter their communion with Jehovah and with one another. The most significant feature of the ceremony was the sprinkling of the blood of the sacrifices. Half of this blood was poured on the altar, and half was sprinkled on the people, but not until the *"Book of the Covenant"* had been read to them and they again had made their solemn promise: "All that the Lord hath said will we do, and be obedient." "Then Moses took the blood and sprinkled it on the people and said, Behold the blood of the covenant, which the Lord hath made with you concerning all these words." The fact that half the blood was poured on the altar and half on the people indicated that both parties were in fellowship and bound themselves to keep the terms of the covenant, the people promising obedience, and Jehovah promising help and blessing.

The sealing of the covenant was followed by a sacrificial feast. Such a ceremonial meal was always regarded as a symbol of communion with God. The participants were Moses and the representatives of Israel; the place was on Mount Sinai. This feast was signalized above all others by a vision of God Himself, not now in thunder and lightning and smoke and fire, but in a scene of exquisite loveliness, standing on clear sapphire, "blue as the blue of heaven." It is idle to speculate on the mode of this manifestation. No visible form was presented to the eye, but in the solemn act of worship they realized the divine presence. The covenant had been sealed with blood. They now had no fear. "They saw

God and did eat and drink." They were guests at His board. It requires no imagination to interpret this scene to those who, under the New Covenant, have been sprinkled with the blood of the True Sacrifice, who have all boldness in the presence of God, and enjoy fellowship with Him, and catch a new vision of His glory in the face of Jesus Christ.

MOSES ASCENDS THE MOUNTAIN. [Ch. 24:12-18.]

After the sacrificial feast which followed the ratification of the covenant, Moses was summoned to ascend still higher, to the very top of the mountain. Part of the way he was accompanied by his associate Joshua. Then for forty days and forty nights he was alone with God. The scene was one of impressive majesty. "A cloud covered the mount. And the glory of the Lord abode upon Mount Sinai. . . . And the sight of the glory of the Lord was like devouring fire on the top of the mount in the eyes of the children of Israel. And Moses went into the midst of the cloud, and gat him up into the mount." He was on a glorious mission. To him were to be given not only the Tables of Stone, but minute instructions for the erection of the Tabernacle and regulations for all the rites and ceremonies which were to constitute the sacred ritual of the people of God. It would be impossible to exaggerate the influence on the character and career of the Hebrew nation produced by the ceremonial which Moses was instructed to establish, and of equal importance is the spiritual enrichment of the followers of Christ which in type and symbol these divine instructions were destined to impart.

IV

THE TABERNACLE EXODUS 25 to 40

DIRECTIONS FOR ITS CONSTRUCTION. [Chs. 25 to 31.]

THREE surprises meet the reader who begins a study of the Tabernacle, one is its limited dimensions, one its unusual purpose, a third its wealth of typical teaching. The size was hardly larger than a single room in many modern homes. The purpose of this "Tent of Meeting" was to provide a place, not where fellow worshippers could meet, but where representatives of the people could meet with God. Its structure and furniture were symbolic. It is this third feature which constitutes its abiding interest and value, but which presents also its principle problems to the interpreter. There is a danger, on the one hand, of regarding the Tabernacle as merely an object of antiquarian research. On the other hand, there is a temptation to assign to the most insignificant detail of the structure some deep religious import. One should observe the vital difference between spiritual insight and unbridled imagination. Two questions should be kept in mind, first, What did the ritual mean to the Hebrew worshipper? and, second, What should any of its features signify to a follower of Christ? Undoubtedly the answers would have much in common. The Tabernacle furnished a permanent object lesson in divine worship. It spoke of the abiding presence of God, of His holiness and grace, of the way by which He could be approached, of the demand for purity, and consecration, and of the necessity of mediation and sacrifice and intercession. How far these were understood by the Israelites may be uncertain. For the Christian, however, there is a rather definite norm of interpretation: whatever is clearly indicated in the New Testament to have been symbolic and typical in the ancient ritual should be eagerly accepted and cherished, but one should ever be on his guard against allowing mere fancy or traditional analogies to translate supposed resemblances into religious dogmas. The interpretation of types requires great humility and restraint.

The Tabernacle, as erected by Moses, was a rectangular structure or tent, composed of a wooden framework with coverings of cloth and skins. It contained two rooms separated by a heavy veil. The eastern room, the sanctuary, or the Holy Place, was twenty cubits (or thirty feet) in length, ten cubits in height and width; it contained the golden candlestick, the table of shewbread and the altar of incense. The second room, the Holy of Holies, measuring ten cubits in every direction, contained the ark and the mercy seat. This tent stood in an open court, likewise rectangular in shape, one hundred cubits in length and fifty cubits in breadth; it was enclosed by curtains of fine linen, supported by pillars, five cubits in height, filleted with silver, resting in sockets of brass. The court contained the brazen altar and the laver. Into this court priests and worshippers could come to offer sacrifices upon the altar. The sanctuary only priests could enter. Into the Holy of Holies the high priest alone could come, and he only on one day of the year, the Great Day of Atonement.

Standing as it did, in the center of the encampment, the Tabernacle represented to the tribes of Israel, the House of their God, the Dwelling Place of their King, the Pavilion of their Leader. This was indicated most impressively by the Cloud of Glory which rested on the Holy of Holies, day and night, and filled it with the light of the manifested presence of God.

The Christian Church has always regarded the Tabernacle as typifying the person and work of Christ. So John states that the "Word," when incarnate, "dwelt among us," or "dwelt in a tabernacle among us" (John 1:14), meaning that this divine Being had taken up His abode in a human body. In a study of the Tabernacle the supreme purpose should be to discoved in the main features, not in the minor details of the structure, some clear revelation of the glory of Christ.

The Materials. (Ch. 25:1-9). In directing Moses to construct the Tabernacle there is an introductory statement as to the purpose of the structure, its materials, and the pattern to be followed. The *purpose* is this: "Let them make me a sanctuary, that I may dwell among them." Strictly speaking, "the most High dwelleth not in temples made with hands" (Acts 7:48), that is, He is not confined to them, He is not comprehended by them. Nevertheless, He does manifest Himself in especial manner in such places. As men engage in worship, the presence of God becomes more real to them, and the place of worship is for them a "house of God" or a dwelling place of God. In the Tabernacle, God vouchsafed to Israel a visible manifestation of His presence in the "bright cloud" which rested on the holy structure. The sight of the sanctuary reminded the people that God did "dwell among them."

The *materials* to be used were such as would be most available. Precious metals would be found among the ancestral wealth inherited from such patriarchs as Abraham and Joseph. Blue, purple, and scarlet cloth and "fine linen" would be woven by the women; hair and skins would be furnished by the flocks and herds; beautiful red leather was made of sheep skins ("rams' skins dyed red"), and tough material for the outer covering was found in the skins of "badgers," seals, or other sea-animals. The framework was made from the acacia (shittim) wood of the wilderness. Oil and spices would not be difficult to secure for the light, incense and other sacred uses, while the personal treasures of the people could supply the necessary jewels for the vestments of the high priest.

All these materials were, indeed, the voluntary gifts of the people, according to the divine direction: "Bring me an offering: of every man that giveth it willingly with his heart ye shall take my offering." The people were poor. They were recently escaped from slavery, yet it is estimated that the materials of the Tabernacle amounted to the value of hundreds of thousands of dollars. The worship of God must be spiritual, yet He does sanction the erection of beautiful structures for such worship, and these should be provided by the voluntary, if sacrificial, gifts of the people.

The *pattern* for the Tabernacle and its furniture was given by God to Moses: "After the pattern of the tabernacle and the pattern of all the instruments thereof even so shall ye make it." This does not denote a physical model which was to be followed. On the mountain, during those forty days of fellowship with God, Moses was divinely directed as to the most fitting way of worship and as to the structure and ritual by which worship could best be expressed. How far the forms were suggested by Moses' previous knowledge and experience, how far they were the original expressions of ideas divinely inspired, it is useless to inquire. The great reality as to the "pattern" shown by Moses on the mountain is this: The Tabernacle was intended to set forth truths as to the worship of God, given for the instruction of Israel but also for the guidance of the people of God in all ages and places.

The Ark and the Mercy Seat. (Ch. 25:10-22). The two most sacred and significant objects in the Tabernacle are the first to be mentioned. These are the Ark of the Covenant and the mercy seat. While vitally related they are separately described and are to be regarded as distinct.

The *ark* was a small chest or box, constructed of acacia wood which was overlaid with gold. It was some forty inches in length and twenty-seven in depth and width. At the four lower corners were rings of gold through which staves or poles, covered with gold, were inserted. By these staves the ark was to be carried. They were never removed so that the ark was ever ready to be transported. The primary purpose of the ark was to contain the two tables of the Law which were graven on stone "by the finger of God." As this law was the basis of the covenant between Jehovah and Israel, the ark was known as the Ark of the Covenant. It is significant that the commandments were in the most sacred place of worship, as there can be no real worship unless one is mindful of the revealed will of God and eager to relate himself to that will. So too it is to be noted that the ark always was ready to be moved. So true worshippers ever should be ready to go forward following the guidance of God.

The *mercy seat* formed the lid or cover of the ark. It was a plate of solid gold which was kept in its place by the rim or moulding which projected above the top edge of the ark. At each end of the mercy seat was a cherub moulded out of the same mass of gold. These cherubim faced each other with outstretched wings and bowed heads. They overshadowed the mercy seat and formed a canopy for this royal throne, for it was there "between the cherubim" that the Shekinah, or visible manifestation of God, rested. Therefore, it is not too much to say that the mercy seat was the supreme feature of the Tabernacle and of the Mosaic ritual. This was the true meeting place between God and His people. "There I will meet with thee, and I will commune with thee from above the mercy seat, from between the two cherubim which are upon the ark of the testimony" (Ch. 25:22). It was the place of "propitiation," or of "covering" or expiation of sins. On the Great Day of Atonement, the High Priest entered the Holy of Holies with the blood of sacrifice, which he sprinkled on and before the mercy seat, thus making atonement for his own sins and the sins of the nation. It is easy, thereefore, to see depicted here the atonement wrought once for all by Christ, who "is not entered into the holy places made with hands . . . but into heaven itself, now to appear in the presence of God for us" (Heb. 9:24).

The symbol of "covering" or of "propitiation" is clearly applied also to Christ (in Rom. 3:25), "whom God hath set forth to be a *propitiation* through faith in his blood." As we worship in His name we do well to bow in adoration as did the cherubim, which seemed to represent reverence and ready obedience to the divine will. If the ark, with its tables of the Law, represents the holiness of God, the mercy seat is a memorial of His grace.

The Table of Shewbread. (Ch. 25:23-30). Turning from the Holy of Holies to the sanctuary or holy place, we find three articles of furniture, the *table of shewbread* (vs. 23-30), the *golden candlestick* (vs. 31-40) and the *altar of incense* (Ch. 30:1-10). The shewbread ("bread of the presence") consisted of twelve unleavened loaves, one for each of the tribes of Isreal. These were kept continually in the Presence of God. Fresh loaves were substituted every Sabbath day, and the old loaves were eaten by the priests in the holy place. The table on which this bread was placed was made of acacia wood overlaid with gold. It was only large enough to contain the twelve loaves, being three feet long, eighteen inches in width, and twenty-seven inches in height. It was constructed with rings for the rods by which it was carried. It was supplied with "dishes" for conveying the bread and to contain the incense and wine which indicated the bread to be an offering. Such indeed it was, for the real significance seems to be attached not to the table, nor to the weekly disposition of the loaves, but to the bread itself. This was a thank offering, set continually before the Lord, acknowledging His protection and favor, and representing and sanctifying the daily service of His people. The fact, however, that the bread was eaten by the priests in the holy place has been taken to signify that while we perform all our daily tasks in the presence of the Lord, and present to Him all the fruits of our labor, He graciously supplies us with all that is needed for our daily nourishment and support. It is possible to find in the shewrbread a type of Christ. He rendered in the presence of His Father perfect obedience. He is for the world the "bread of life."

The Golden Candlestick. (Ch. 25:31-40). The *candlestick,* or more properly the *lampstand,* consisted of a central perpendicular shaft, from which, on each side, sprang three curved arms or branches. These were all in the same plane and rose to the same level. The shaft and the branches were all ornamented with representations of flowers and pomegranates and lily blossoms. On the top ornament, which was in every case a lily blossom, rested a lamp, in the shape of a bowl or saucer. The entire candlestick was beaten out of pure gold, and while probably of no great size its cost is estimated at many thousands of dollars. For the use of the candlestick special oil was prepared (Ex. 27:20; Lev. 24:2). Indeed, it is this use of oil which distinguishes a lamp from a candle, and gives its symbolic meaning to the lampstand of the holy place. This candlestick was a type of the people of God. Israel of old and the Church today have been appointed to give to the world the light of the knowledge of God. This is possible only by the indwelling Spirit of God, of which Spirit oil is the scriptural symbol. In the Old Testament there is a vision in which Israel is represented by a candlestick to which oil is being supplied abundantly. The inspired message of encouragement to the people of God was this: "Not by might, nor by power, but by my spirit, saith the Lord of hosts" (Zech. 4:6). So in the New Testament, John records his impressive vision. The whole Church is represented by "seven golden candlesticks." In the midst of the "candlesticks" walks the Son of God, by whom life and light are imparted to His Church. As of old the high priest dressed the lamps daily, so Christ is seen correcting, instructing, and warning the several churches as they need. It is the great privilege of a Christian and of the Church to give light in a world of darkness. This is possible only by the presence and power of the Holy Spirit. Christ is Himself "the light of the world." To His was given the Spirit "without measure." His followers can perform their blessed function of being lights in this world only as they are yielded to His service to do His will, and consequently are filled with His Spirit.

The Coverings. (Ch. 26:1-14). It is probable that in all ancient literature no structure is described with more minuteness and exactness than the Tabernacle erected by Moses. There still remain, however, certain questions as to its construction and its typical teachings which cannot be answered with absolute certainty. One cause of divergent views is found in the fact that the term "Tabernacle" is used at times to include not only the sacred tent but also its surrounding court. Then, again, a distinction is drawn between the "Taber-

nacle" and the "Tent." It will be remembered that
there were four "coverings" over the holy place and the
Holy of Holies, one of "fine linen," one of "goats' hair,"
one of "rams' skins," and one of "badgers' skins." The
word "Tabernacle," in this connection, is understood to
apply only to the covering of "fine" linen" (vss. 1-6),
and the word "tent" to the covering of goats' hair (vss.
7-13). In this view it is further supposed that the structure was erected with a ridge pole. This raised the
"tent" of "goats' hair tent cloth" some distance above
"the tabernacle" in the form of a roof, over which were
spread the coverings of "rams' skins" and "badgers'
skins." This debatable question is of no great importance, and as for any symbolism, the different coverings
were designed less for spiritual instruction than for prac-
tical purposes. The "Tabernacle," or "Dwelling," which
included both the holy place and the Holy of Holies,
was hung with curtains made of linen thread ornamented with woven figures of cherubim. These figures
were symbolic of the holiness of God. This "tabernacle
cloth" is what is meant in verse 6 by "one tabernacle,"
for these ten breadths of cloth or "curtains" were furnished with loops and "taches" so that all could be
united in one great covering. It did, however, have two
divisions, composed of five curtains each. The two were
united by the loops and taches, but could easily be
separated when the structure was to be moved. This
superb covering of purple, blue, and scarlet, with its
ornaments of cherubim, was, in all, forty cubits long and
twenty-eight wide.

    The second covering, or the "tent," was of goats'
hair cloth and was spread over or above the "tabernacle"

of "fine linen." This, like the first, was in two portions, each made of several "breadths," or "curtains," but of these one was composed of five breadths and one of six. This covering was six feet broader than the inner one, which, for its protection, was overlapped at both ends by this goats' hair cloth.

The two outer coverings were of rams' skins, and seal or badger skins. They were evidently designed not merely to keep out the light, but to protect the sacred shrine from sun and wind and rain, and to provide a structure which easily could be dismantled and transported from place to place as the movable dwelling place of the King.

The Framework. (Ch. 26:15-30). The elaborate coverings of the Tabernacle were supported by a wooden framework. This was made of boards of acacia wood overlaid with gold. There were forty-eight of these boards, twenty for the south and twenty for the north side and eight for the west end. They were placed upright and were held together laterally by transverse bars of gold-covered acacia wood. At the lower end of each board were two "tenons," or hands, which were sunk into two corresponding holes or mortices in sockets of silver. These sockets, or bases, formed the foundation of the Tabernacle. They were massive blocks of silver, each weighing more than eighty pounds. Probably they were deeply imbedded in the ground. To provide these sockets the Israelites contributed one hundred talents of silver. This was a costly foundation, and its value must have been at least two hundred thousand dollars. The silver was described as "atonement money" (Ch. 30:16).

Thus this portable temple rested on a foundation which may have reminded the worshippers that they were a ransomed and a redeemed people.

The Veil and Curtain. (Ch. 26:31-36). The boards of acacia wood not merely supported the rich coverings of the Tabernacle but formed the walls of the structure, which was, in effect, a room forty-five feet in length and fifteen feet in breadth, of which the boards were the walls and the curtains of fine linen were the ceiling. The room was divided by a veil, or curtain, into two compartments: first, the holy place, which contained the table of shewbread, the candlestick, and the altar of incense, and, second, the Holy of Holies, in which was the ark. This veil was made of the same fine linen as was the ceiling and it likewise was ornamented with figures of cherubim, symbolizing the presence and holiness and majesty of God. Its very colors were impressive and to them special significance has been attached. They are mentioned elsewhere as characteristic features of all the hangings. Blue has been regarded as symbolizing heavenly beauty; purple as a sign of royalty; scarlet as related to sacrifice, and "fine linen" as picturing holiness.

At the east end of the Tabernacle there was another veil forming the door or entrance to the holy place. This likewise was of fine linen but apparently not adorned with cherubim. The veil which separated the holy place and the Holy of Holies was the most sacred and significant of all the curtains and hangings of the Tabernacle. The priests could pass freely the first veil to serve in the outer sanctuary, but the second veil only the high priest could pass and only on one day of the year. This provision did prefigure the atoning work of Christ, our Great High Priest, yet it also indicated a restriction which characterized the Old Dispensation (Heb. 9:8, 9). Christ has made free and immediate access to God possible for all believers. At the instant of His death "the veil of the Temple was rent in twain from the top to the bottom" (Mark 15:38). This was a historic fact; it was also a typical and significant event. By His atoning work Christ has opened "a new and living way, which he hath consecrated for us, through the veil, that is to say, his flesh" (Heb. 10:20), so that now, with no restriction as to time or place or person, all who trust and follow Him can enter the Holy of Holies into the immediate presence of God, and can "come boldly unto the throne of grace" to "obtain mercy and find grace to help in time of need."

The Altar of Burnt Offering. (Ch. 27:1-8). Real worship involves sacrifice: access to God is by way of propitiation and pardon; fellowship is made possible by atonement. Thus the first object which met the sight of the worshipper as he entered the court of the Tabernacle was an altar. It was called the altar of burnt offering because of the prominence of this form of offering in the sacrificial system. It was known also as the brazen altar, as it was covered with brass or bronze, and the various vessels, or utensils, used in the service were likewise of bronze. Thus it was distinguished from the golden altar on which incense was burned.

The brazen altar was built of acacia boards. It was seven feet and a half in length and breadth and four feet and a half in height. Apparently it was a hollow casing filled with earth or stones. The "compass" of the altar (vs. 6) is supposed to have been a projecting step or platform, running around the outside and midway its height, on which the priests stood to officiate. The "horns" of the altar were projections at the four corners. They were of the same piece with the altar itself and not merely added ornaments. As to their shape and significance considerable difference of view exists. Many regard them as symbols of power and protection. They were sprinkled with the same blood that was sprinkled at the mercy seat and on the horns of the golden altar. Persons fleeing for refuge were regarded as safe when clinging to these horns. Thus they were connected with the whole ritual and are related to that atoning work of Christ typified by sacrifice and priesthood and altar. As the apostle declares, "We have an altar" (Heb. 13:10). The cross of Christ has become for us the symbol of His salvation. He is our Priest, our Altar, our Sacrifice. We need no other altar. We have been "reconciled to God" by His cross. Through Him we have access to the Father. By the way of this Altar we can pass on to the Laver, to the Altar of Incense, to the Mercy Seat in the Holy of Holies, to the presence of the living God.

However, we must remember that the burnt offering was a symbol of complete dedication. To pass that altar means that we yield ourselves wholly to the service of God, and follow in His footsteps who came not to do His own will but the will of His Father in absolute submission and self-sacrificing love.

The Court of the Tabernacle. (Ch. 27:9-19). A follower of Christ has immediate and unrestricted access to God in all places and at all times. However, an ideal place of worship is characterized by something of seclusion, of isolation and retirement. One wishes to have the world shut out, and to be shut in alone with God. With this law in mind our Saviour could say: "When thou prayest enter into thy closet, and when thou hast shut thy door, pray to thy Father which is in secret." Accordingly, the Tabernacle of Israel, when pitched in the midst of the twelve tribes, was surrounded by a court which secluded the worshippers from the busy life of the camp. This sacred court was seventy-five feet in breadth and one hundred and fifty feet in length. It was open to the sky, and was enclosed by curtains woven of linen thread and suspended from pillars, or graceful columns, standing upright in sockets of brass. The height of these pillars was seven feet six inches, and they stood seven feet six inches apart. They were connected at their tops by silver rods and were furnished with silver hooks to which the hangings were attached, and their capitals were overlaid with silver. On three sides of this court there was no entrance or gateway, but on the east side the line of hangings was broken in the middle. A space of thirty feet was left to be covered by an immense screen of fine twined linen in blue purple and scarlet. This curtain could be drawn up and down and was designed to give admission to the court. The only objects placed in this enclosure which surrounded the Tabernacle proper were the brazen altar and the laver. The statement that "all the vessels of the Tabernacle" were of brass (vs. 19) refers rather to the utensils and the tent pins which previously had not been mentioned. Much of the other furnishings had been described as made of silver and gold, particularly those of the sacred tent. Into this tent, with its holy place and its Holy of Holies, only the priests could enter, but all Israelites were freely admitted to the court by which it was enclosed.

The Oil for the Lamps. (Ch. 27:20, 21). The lamps of the golden candlestick were to be lighted every evening and extinguished every morning. For their use special olive oil was to be prepared. It was to be of the very best kind. It was called "beaten" oil because it was prepared by merely bruising fresh olives in a mortar. The inferior oil was secured by subjecting unselected fruit to stronger pressure and the application of heat. The "beaten" oil would be free from the various impurities found in oil crushed in a mill after the ordinary method. Thus the proverbial phrase "beaten oil" should describe the product, not of unusual labor, but of special care, and most specifically a product characterized by peculiar purity. This oil for the lamps is, therefore, a proper symbol of the Holy Spirit, whose indwelling power enables the people of God to illumine the darkness of this world with the light of the knowledge of the glory and grace revealed in Christ the Lord.

The Priestly Garments. (Ch. 28:1-43). The official dress of the high priest was most elaborate and is minutely described. Made of the richest materials and of the most brilliant colors, bordered with golden bells, bearing on its mitre the solemn inscription, "Holiness to the Lord," it is probable that no more splendid and imposing apparel has been worn by any leader of religious worship. However, the real significance of these priestly garments lies in their typical character in view of the fact that the office of Aaron and his sons was symbolic of the person and work of Christ who, in the New Testament, and particularly in the Epistle to the Hebrews, is set forth as our Great High Priest.

Of these priestly garments seven are mentioned: the ephod, breastplate, robe, mitre, coat, girdle, and linen drawers. All may be of interest, but two or three demand special study.

The *ephod* was the outermost garment. It was made of two pieces of cloth, one for the front and one for the back, joined together by straps at the shoulders. These straps were clasped firmly by two large onyx stones. The garment was costly and magnificent, being made of gold thread, and of "blue and purple and scarlet and fine twined linen." The principal feature, however, were the onyx gems which rested on the shoulders of the priest. On these were engraved the names of the twelve tribes of Israel. This was to indicate that the high priest represented all the people, in the presence of God, even as Christ is declared "to appear in the presence of God for us."

The *breastplate* was the most costly and the most conspicuous of the priestly garments. It was made of the same material as the ephod, about nine inches square, and so folded or "doubled" as to form a bag or pocket. It was fastened to the ephod, above and below, by rings and chains of gold. Upon the linen groundwork were fastened twelve jewels, set in an open work of gold, and arranged in three rows, four in each row. On each one of these gems was engraved the name of one of the twelve tribes of Israel. Thus not only upon his shoulders, but upon his heart the high priest bore the names of the people for whose sake he served and in whose behalf he wore the priestly robe. Thus Christ our Great High Priest bears on His shoulder and on His heart the names of those who belong to Him. They can ever be assured of His sustaining grace and His everlasting love. They may be conscious of their unworthiness or despised by an unfriendly world, but to the Saviour they are all precious jewels whom He gladly presents in the presence of a holy God.

Within the fold or pocket of the breastplate were two small mysterious objects, the *urim* and *thummin*. Their real character is extremely uncertain, but it seems that by them in some unknown manner the will of God was made plain to His people through their representative, the high priest.

The *mitre* formed the headdress of the priestly attire. It was a species of turban, made of several folds of white linen. Its only ornament was a plate of pure gold, but it was the conspicuous feature of the mitre to which it was attached by a blue band or fillet. The plate bore this inscription: "Holiness to the Lord." It taught the lesson that the very crown of all worship and of all religion is holiness. We are reminded of the perfect holiness of our Great High Priest, in whom we are "accepted," whose righteousness is imputed to us, and who ever encourages us to "follow . . . holiness without which no man shall see the Lord."

It is interesting to note that holiness is also the

message of the inner garments provided for Aaron and also for his sons. Of these little is said. They included for each one a tunic, drawers, and a girdle. They were of white linen, a symbol of "the righteousness of saints."

These various priestly garments were "for glory and beauty," but they were symbolic. They are not to be reproduced in physical attire to be worn by worshippers today. They were types of spiritual realities. They find their true antitypes in the virtues and excellencies and saving grace of Christ, and they indicate the supreme need of holiness on the part of all who follow in His steps and bear His name.

The Consecration of the Priests. (Ch. 29:1-46). The record of the ceremonial here prescribed is set forth more fully in Leviticus (Chs. 8 and 9) and with particular reference to the law of the offerings (Lev. 1-7). The four principal features of the ritual were (1) ablution, (2) investiture, (3) anointing, (4) sacrifice. In this service of consecration Aaron and his sons were united, but the pre-eminence is given to the high priest. Typically they represented Christ and His followers, for believers form a universal priesthood and are consecrated to the service of God.

(1) The washing with water symbolized the need of purity on the part of all who are to engage in divine worship or in daily service. The high priest was to be in symbol what Christ was in reality, holy and free from sin. So, too, all believers need to be cleansed at the laver (Titus 3:5) before they are ready for their priestly service among men.

(2) Investiture followed. First, Aaron was to be

clothed with the garments of "glory and beauty" described in the previous chapter; and then, after his anointing, his sons were to put on the white linen prescribed for them. This typified the radiant character of Christ, and the holiness required of all believers.

(3) The anointing with sacred oil symbolized the graces and gifts of the Holy Spirit. This was the prime feature of the consecration. On the head of Aaron this precious oil was poured in profusion, as described in Psalm 133:2. It was sprinkled on all of his sons. So the Holy Spirit was given to Christ without measure (John 3:34). Yet His presence and power are granted to all who truly belong to Him. (Rom. 8:9).

(4) The sacrifice included the whole round of Levitical offerings. Taken together, they represent self-surrender to God on the part of those for whom they are presented. This is the very essence of consecration. However, first of all, there was the *sin offering*. Its blood was shed in expiation, and the body was "burned without the camp" (Heb. 13:11-13). Then a *burnt offering* was presented, all of which was consumed on the altar, as propitiation should be succeeded by complete dedication to God (vss. 15-18). Next followed the *peace offering* in the form of "the ram of consecration." Part of this sacrifice was burned on the altar, as belonging to God; part was taken by the priests, waved toward the altar, and then taken back by the priests as the portion to be eaten by them. This expressed communion with God as the issue of consecration to Him. Last of all was the *meat offering*, or, more exactly, the "meal offering," represented by the unleavened bread, the oiled cake, and

the wafer (vs. 23) and symbolizing the dedication to God of all the fruits of one's labor.

This complete consecration was further typified by touching the ear, the hand, and the foot of each priest with blood of the sacrifice, and by sprinkling Aaron and his sons with blood and oil. That is, all that they were and all that they did belonged to God. So believers have been redeemed by precious blood and anointed by the Holy Spirit for service.

After directing that the altar itself was to be consecrated with blood, provision was made for the establishment of a *daily sacrifice*, and a promise was given of the *continual presence of God*. The sacrifice was to consist of two lambs, one offered in the morning and one in the evening. These were partly in expiation of the daily sins of the people, and partly as a sign of renewed dedication to God. They were accompanied by "meal" and "drink" offerings, which were in grateful recognition of God's daily mercies, of His loving kindness and protecting care. In the lives of Christians there should be something corresponding to this morning and evening sacrifice of thanksgiving and dedication. Those thus consecrated can claim for themselves the promise with which the directions for the consecration of Aaron and his sons is brought to a close: "And I will dwell among the children of Israel and be their God." The whole purpose of this ritual of consecration has been declared to be a testimony to the fact that a people delivered from bondage by the power of God might be consecrated to Him in daily life and dwell continually in His presence.

The Altar of Incense. (Ch. 30:1-19). A possible explanation has been given of the fact that until now no mention has been made of the altar of incense. It might naturally have been described in connection with the other articles of furniture, the ark, the candlestick, the table of shewbread, the altar of brass, at least before the chapters dealing with the priestly garments and the consecration of the priests. The explanation given is this: incense is the symbol of *worship*, and no worship could be offered without a sacrifice, and no sacrifice without a priest. When an altar of burnt-offering had been provided, when a priesthood had been consecrated, then an altar should be ready for the offering of incense. The main design of the Tabernacle and its rites was worship, or communion with the living God who dwelt among His chosen people. Therefore, the whole section of Exodus, beginning with the description of the ark (Ch. 25:1), reaches its climax with the provision of an altar of incense (Ch. 30:1-10). This is in accordance with the law: "That which is first in design is last in execution." This altar of incense was to be of the same shape as the brazen altar but much smaller, only eighteen inches square and three feet in height. It was to be of the same material as the brazen altar, that is, of boards of acacia wood, but covered with plates of gold, and, next to the ark, it was the most sacred article of furniture connected with the Tabernacle. At the four corners horns projected upward, and on the two sides were golden rings, through which the staves were to be put when the altar was carried from place to place as the camp was moved.

The position of the altar is significant. It stood

outside the veil but immediately before the mercy seat, which was in the Holy of Holies directly opposite. Although the veil interposed, the altar was spoken of as before the ark, as if nothing intervened—"the altar which is before the Lord" (Lev. 4:18). It sustained a more intimate connection with the Holy of Holies than did the candlestick or the table of shewbread, which also were in the Holy Place. Indeed, in the Epistle to the Hebrews it is referred to as belonging to the Holy of Holies (9:4). The altar of incense was closely related to the ark and the mercy seat, to the cloud of glory, to the manifested presence of God.

It symbolized communion with God in worship, in praise, and in prayer. This is made possible for believers by the mediation of Christ. He is at once the Offering and the Priest. We need no others. "By Him" we may "offer the sacrifice of praise to God continually; that is, the fruit of our lips giving thanks in His name" (Heb. 13:15). Incense is surely the type of the prayers of God's people (Rev. 5:8). This golden altar was, therefore, the place of intercession. The scene in Revelation (8:3-5) represents the prayers of the saints in heaven, or, as many suppose, the intercession of Christ Himself, as mingling with the prayers of the "saints" on earth and ascending before God in petition and in adoration.

However, all human worship is imperfect; therefore it was necessary for the high priest, once every year, to make atonement for the altar itself. He must touch the horns of the golden altar with the blood of sacrifice. So while "we know not what we should pray for as we ought," and while conscious of our unworthiness to approach the mercy seat, we believe that we are "accepted in the beloved," because of His atoning blood and His unfailing intercession for us (Eph. 1:6, 7; Rom. 8:34; Heb. 9:25).

The Ransom Money. (Ch. 30:11-16). Only the redeemed could worship, or in the person of their representative, the priest, could draw near to the Golden Altar. This was impressed deeply on the minds of the Israelites by the requirement that, when a census was taken, everyone over twenty years of age must pay into the sacred treasury a half shekel known as ransom money: "They shall give, every man, a ransom for his soul unto the Lord." This was to indicate that he was unworthy to be numbered among the people of the Lord and to enjoy all of His mercies. In some way, atonement should be made for every man. Therefore, it was appointed that this specified price should be paid as a symbol and pledge of his redemption. The same amount was required of each one: "The rich shall not give more, and the poor shall not give less than half a shekel, when they give an offering unto the Lord, to make an atonement for your souls." This was a divine declaration that all persons are of equal value in the sight of God. Rich and poor, learned and ignorant, bond or free, all are treated as equals, all alike are unworthy of the place given them among the redeemed people of God, all require the same expiation. This truth as to the need of redemption was kept constantly in the minds of the worshippers, for while all other materials required to construct the Tabernacle were free-will offerings, all the silver employed came from the ransom money which was required of each one enrolled among the redeemed people. Thus it is with the followers of Christ. They are exhorted by Peter to live lives of holiness on the ground that for them a ransom has been paid. They form a ransomed people. "They are not redeemed with corruptible things as silver and gold . . . but with the precious blood of Christ as of a lamb without blemish and without spot" (I Peter 1:18, 19). In recognition of this redemption they offer lives of purity and love and godly fear.

The Laver. (Ch. 30:17-21). The approach to God in worship requires not only redemption but also cleansing. There is need of holiness as well as propitiation. Thus in the court of the tabernacle, between the altar of burnt offering and the entrance to the Holy Place, stood the *laver.* It was made of brass, or bronze, supplied by metal mirrors contributed for this purpose by women who came to the tabernacle to worship. The size or shape of this laver is unknown. Mention of its "foot" has led to the belief that it was in the form of a large vase or urn supported by a slender stem which rose from a pedestal.

At this laver, under pain of death, every priest must wash before offering a sacrifice or entering into the holy place.

The message for the worshipper is quite clear. Water is an accepted symbol of the word, or truth, of God. As applied to the soul by the Holy Spirit, sin is washed away and a new life begins. Thus Paul speaks of "the washing [laver] of regeneration and renewing of the Holy Ghost" (Titus 3:5). However, while regeneration, or justification, is once and for all, yet cleansing or sanctification is needed daily. One who has been "bathed needeth not save to wash his feet but is clean every whit." We do need daily cleansing from daily defilement. Those who have been "bathed" at the "laver" need to be cleansed for every priestly act. One who has been regenerated at the laver needs not to be "bathed" again, but he does need to have the stains washed away which he has contracted as he walked even on his way to the place of service or of sacrifice (John 13:1-10).

The Anointing Oil. (Ch. 30:22-33). The priests who ministered in the Tabernacle needed to be anointed with sacred oil before entering on their service. The followers of Christ form a universal priesthood. They, too, need to be anointed by the Holy Spirit for all their work and worship. The oil used for the anointing of Aaron and his sons was known as "the holy anointing oil". It was composed, according to a very minute prescription, of myrrh, cinnamon, calamus, and cassia. These four precious spices were symbolic of the gifts and graces of the Holy Spirit granted for Christian life and service. It is obvious, therefore, why this oil was not allowed to be used by any private person nor for any common purpose. However, with this oil "the tabernacle was to be anointed, and the ark, and the table, the candlestick, the altar of incense, the altar of burnt offering and the laver," which indicates that Christians do receive special spiritual graces, and that there is a particular sacredness attached to their places of worship and to all their daily tasks, to their persons and their possessions (II Cor. 1:21; I John 2:20, 27).

The Incense. (Ch. 30:34-38). The incense to be used in the Tabernacle, like the holy anointing oil, was to be composed of four aromatic ingredients—stacte, onycha, galbanum, and frankincense. It was to be carefully prepared, and put to no common use; nor be employed by any person except the priests. A portion was to be put outside the veil but near the golden altar on which it was to be burnt. It was thus especially associated with the ark and said to be "before the testimony." While the oil was called "holy," the incense was styled "most holy." All of these provisions denote the sacredness and dignity and reverence to be associated with the worship of God. This ever is symbolized by the incense which was offered on the golden altar. Its fragrance rose in the very presence of God, who was manifested in the Holy of Holies beyond the veil.

The Builders. (Ch. 31:1-11). Full instructions now have been given to Moses for the construction of the Tabernacle and all its furniture. Moses, however, was not an artist or a builder. Therefore, the names of two men divinely appointed and equipped to undertake and direct the work were given him. These were Bezaleel of the tribe of Judah and Aholiab of the tribe of Dan. The former seems to have been the chief artificer in metal, stone, and wood, and to have acquired the "art of the apothecary" for compounding the anointing oil and the incense. Aholiab, on the other hand, seems to have been responsible for all the textile work, in connection with which there are here enumerated the richly adorned robes of the high priest and the garments of white linen for all the priests.

In connection with the appointment of these two
workmen, all the articles of furniture are again named,
and in the same order as before, only here the altar of
incense is named in connection with the candlestick
and the table of shewbread. In mentioning the appointment of Aholiab the divine message is given: "I have
filled him with the spirit of God," in connection with
which a strange theory has been formed, relative to the
operation of the Holy Spirit, according to which it is
held that in Old Testament times the Spirit of God
operated in the lives of only exceptional men, such as
prophets, priests, and kings, and also these builders of
the Tabernacle. The truth is that, in all ages, the self-
same Spirit has been operating in all the people of God,
regenerating, sanctifying, and instructing them; yet He
has given special abilities and talents according to the
work to which they have been called. His inspiration
does not supersede normal human faculties, nor is His
influence confined to those whose work is spiritual or
even intellectual in character. The same blessed Com-
forter is present with every servant of God at all times,
for every task and experience of life. He is as ready to
guide and help the most obscure worker who is em-
broidering a design on a curtain which is to be unseen as
He is to aid the artist who is fashioning the golden plate
for the mitre of the high priest.

The Sabbath. (Ch. 31:12-17). The extensive instructions to Moses for the construction of the Tabernacle having been given, and special workmen having
been appointed for the erection of this sacred place of
worship, a command is added relative to the most sacred

day of worship. Mention of the Sabbath has been made
before, in connection with the gift of manna, and as one
of the Ten Words. The re-enactment of the law here
gives to it a new sanction and sets forth its intention and
value. The solemn sanction was the provision here
made for the inflicton of the death penalty for anyone
who broke the Sabbath law, and the purpose of the observance is clearly set forth as no longer merely obedience to God but as a sacramental sign between God and
His people. So the observance of the Lord's day should
be observed as marking a covenant between Christ and
His followers who should be careful to remember this
day "to keep it holy."

The Tables of Stone. (Ch. 31:18). At the end
of all this instruction relative to the Tabernacle (Chs.
25 to 31), is added the historic statement that the Lord
"gave unto Moses, when he had made an end of com-
muning with him upon mount Sinai, two tables of testimony, tables of stone, written with the finger of God."
These tables represented the covenant between God and
His people. When placed in the ark and covered by the
mercy seat they would give the sanctuary its true significance as a place of worship. The account of the
erection of the Tabernacle is now deferred until a record
is made of the tragic events which occurred in the camp
of Israel while Moses was on the mountain alone with
God.

THE SIN OF THE PEOPLE. [Chs. 32 to 34.]

The Golden Calf. (Ch. 32:1-6). It is difficult to
believe that a people so soon would turn against their

God who had delivered them from cruel bondage, who had brought them through the sea and across the wilderness and had bound them to Himself by a most solemn covenant. It is almost as difficult to believe that they would be so quickly discouraged by the failure of Moses to return, and would speak with so little respect or affection for him, their heroic and devoted leader. However, we read that "when the people saw that Moses delayed to come down out of the mount, the people gathered themselves together unto Aaron, and said unto him, Up, make us gods, which shall go before us; for as for this Moses, the man that brought us up out of the land of Egypt, we wot not what is become of him." It is not quite certain what the people desired. Probably they wished some visible manifestation of God which they could worship and follow. The inclination of the Israelites to idolatry had been manifested even during their bondage in Egypt. In any event, Aaron took the earrings of gold which the people were wearing and made of the metal "a molten calf." Possibly the translation "fashioned it with a graving tool" is open to question. The words may mean that Aaron gathered into a receptacle all those gold ornaments and then melted them in a mold of a young bullock. "He built an altar before it; . . . and said, Tomorrow is a feast to the Lord." It is, therefore, not quite certain whether the sin was a breach of the First or the Second Commandment. If the feast really was to Jehovah, then it disregarded the prohibition against the worship of images. If the object of worship was regarded in itself as a god, then it was a clear breach of the First Commandment. In either case it was a grievous fault. "They rose up early on the morrow, and offered burnt offerings, and brought peace offerings; and the people sat down to eat and to drink, and rose up to play." Their attitude toward Moses and toward God is not so surprising when one remembers how much of ingratitude there is in the human heart and when one recalls that it even was necessary for the Apostle John to warn the early Christians, "Little children, keep yourselves from idols."

The Penalty. (Ch. 32:7-29). When Moses receives a divine intimation of the distressing situation at the foot of the mountain, he first of all pleads with the Lord to spare the people, who are in danger of being consumed by His wrath. He then descends from the mountain with the tables of the testimony in his hand. When he draws near to the camp, and discovers the appalling situation, "He cast the tables out of his hands, and brake them beneath the mount." It was an expression of his indignation at an act of idolatry by which was indicated a breaking of the covenant attested by the tables of stone.

"And he took the calf which they had made, and burnt it in the fire, and ground it to powder, and strawed it upon the water, and made the children of Israel drink of it." When Moses meets his brother he turns to him with bitter irony to ask in what way the people have ever injured him that he, in return, has brought so much evil upon them. The reply of Aaron is so weak and preposterous as to be absurd. He lays the entire fault on the people and then intimates that the creation of the golden calf was merely an accident, "I said unto them, Whosoever hath any gold, let them break it off. So they gave it me: then I cast it into the fire, and there came out this calf." As Moses now witnesses the shameless orgy in which the people were engaged he sounded out the call, "Who is on the Lord's side? Let him come unto me." The first to show their loyalty were the sons of Levi. They were sent through the camp with drawn swords to take vengeance on all who still insisted on their indecent and idolatrous revel; "and there fell of the people that day about three thousand men." This was a severe penalty, but it seemed necessary to rescue the people from being destroyed as a nation of idolaters.

Moses' Intercession. (Chs. 32:30 to 33:23). The sin had been grievous and the penalty was severe, yet the entire nation would have perished, humanly speaking, had it not been for the intercession of Moses. This is sometimes regarded as the most notable act of his career. It has been compared with the prayer of Abraham (Gen. 18), with the high priestly prayer of Christ (John 17), and even with the present intercession of our Lord (Heb. 7:25). Moses had begun the intercession while on the mountain. It expressed supreme unselfishness. The suggestion had been made that Israel might be destroyed and that out of Moses a great nation might arise.

Moses pleads for the people and presents three arguments: First of all, God has done so much for Israel that surely He could not destroy them when He has chosen them as His own and redeemed them by His power. Second, their destruction would he regarded as a triumph by the Egyptians. In the third place, it would nullify the promises made to Abraham, Isaac, and Jacob.

At the request of Moses, the divine sentence is suspended until the punishment has been inflicted. Then Moses ascends the mountain and renews his intercession. It is now that his plea reaches the height of self-abnegation. "And Moses returned unto the Lord, and said, Oh, this people have sinned a great sin, and have made them gods of gold. Yet now, if thou wilt forgive their sin—; and if not, blot me, I pray thee, out of thy book which thou hast written."

The reply of the Lord is to the effect that one man cannot take upon him the sins of another, and unless there is repentance and forgiveness of the offender the penalty must be inflicted. Even the merits of Christ cannot avail unless one turns from sin with detestation and new resolution. However, God promises to spare the people, but He now withdraws the promise of His abiding presence, and He offers instead to send His angel before the people. This announcement brought the deepest distress to the Israelites. As a sign of their repentance and humiliation they stripped off the ornaments which they usually wore, hoping that the former status would be renewed. Meanwhile, Moses erects a temporary tabernacle. He wishes for a place where he can commune with God. The erection of the structure concerning which he has received directions while on the mount would require a delay of many days. Meanwhile, therefore, he makes use of a small tent, which is designated "the tent of meeting." This term is afterwards applied to the Tabernacle when it has been constructed. As he enters this temporary house of God, the pillar of cloud and fire descends upon it, indicating the divine presence. Moses now renews his supplication for the people, urging God to renew His former promise. He receives this gracious reply: "My presence shall be with thee, and I will give thee rest." To this gracious word Moses makes reply, "If thy presence go not with me, carry us not up hence."

Having thus secured for the people pardon and the renewed assurance of the divine leadership, Moses at last makes a request for himself. What he desires above all else is a new and clearer vision of God. He wishes more than he had experienced even on the holy mountain. "And he said, I beseech thee, shew me thy glory." It is difficult to understand exactly what he expected. No man can really see God and live. "No man hath seen God at any time." However, there was granted to Moses a mysterious experience. He saw as real a manifestation of divine glory as has ever been granted to man. He received the divine promise, "I will put thee in a clift of the rock, and will cover thee with my hand while I pass by." It was to be a place of seclusion and protection. There the vision was granted him. As the Lord had said, "My face shall not be seen," but there was revealed an afterglow of the glory which passed by, all the glory, indeed, that it was possible for mortal man to see. This was a notable and noble desire on the part of the great leader. Many have longed for the "vision beatific." "Blessed are the pure in heart, for they shall see God."

The Covenant Renewed. (Ch. 34:1-27). Moses is commanded to ascend the mountain again and to bring with him two new tables of stone, so, early in the morning, he ascends Mount Sinai with the tables of stone in his hand. "And the Lord passed by before him, and proclaimed, The Lord, The Lord God, merciful and gracious, longsuffering and abundant in goodness and truth, keeping mercy for thousands, forgiving iniquity and transgression and sin."

As Moses bows his head he again prays for the continuance of the divine presence, and God shows Himself to be merciful and gracious, as He has proclaimed, by renewing His covenant with the people. He promises to bring them into the land of Canaan and to drive out the nations before them. However, He repeats anew the terms of the covenant. It includes the keeping of the commandments which had been given before, and also the observance of the three annual festivals: the Feast of Passover and Unleavened Bread, the Feast of Weeks or Pentecost, and the Feast of Ingathering or Tabernacles. The observance of the Sabbath is again enjoined and also the redemption of the first-born and the offering to God of the first fruits of the land. In recognition of the renewed covenant God has given the two new tables of the law, with which Moses descends the mountain after his second long period of forty days and forty nights spent in communion with God.

The Shining of Moses' Face. (Ch. 34:28-35). The unfortunate introduction of a single word by the translators has largely obscured from all readers of the Old Testament the real significance of the incident of the shining of Moses' face. According to the narrative, "When Moses came down from mount Sinai with the two tables of testimony in Moses' hand, when he came down from the mount, that Moses wist not that the skin of his face shone while he talked with him. And when Aaron and all the children of Israel saw Moses, behold, the skin of his face shone; and they were afraid to come nigh him. And Moses called unto them; and Aaron and all the rulers of the congregation returned unto him: and Moses talked with them. And afterward all the children of Israel came nigh: and he gave them in commandment all that the Lord had spoken with him in mount Sinai." All this is quite clear and significant. It was not unnatural that after Moses had beheld the glory of the Lord and had spent forty days with the Lord on the mountain that his face shone with a reflected light.

However, the translators now add, "And *till* Moses had done speaking with them he put a veil on his face." The verse should read, "And *when* Moses had done speaking with them he put a veil on his face. But when Moses went in before the Lord to speak with Him, he took the veil off, until he came out. . . . And the children of Israel saw the face of Moses, that the skin of Moses' face shone: and Moses put the veil upon his face again, until he went in to speak with Him."

Therefore, it is clear that Moses did not veil his face to hide the glory from the people. He hid his face so that the people could not see the glory fade away, as it did until Moses went again into the "tent of meeting" and spoke with the Lord. He then came out again with shining face to meet the people.

This more exact statement of the experience of Moses is used by Saint Paul in II Corinthians (3:7-18) to contrast the glory of the Gospel with the glory of the law. Paul insists that the law was glorious, and intimates that when ascending the mountain to receive the law,

Moses was on a glorious mission. It was so glorious that as a result his face shone with a holy light when he descended the mountain with the tables of the law in his hand. However, the glory faded from the face of Moses, which was a symbol that the glory has faded from the law only because of the brighter radiance of the glorious Gospel of Christ. It was a great privilege for a man to receive the Commandments with their unfailing and divine sanctions. This law is still and ever will be the moral code for man, but the law makes us the more conscious of our need of pardon and of power, and of the transforming influence of Christ. Thus Paul contrasts the experience of the Christian, and particularly of the Christian minister, with the experience of Moses who found it necessary to veil his face that the fading of its glory might not be seen. "But we all," writes the apostle, "with open [unveiled] faced beholding as in a glass the glory of the Lord, are changed [transfigured] into the same image from glory to glory, even as by the Spirit of the Lord."

The contrast is very beautiful. The glory of Christian character is not that of a reflected radiance. It comes from within. It results not merely from an attempted imitation of Christ, but it is a transfiguration produced by the power of the indwelling Spirit of Christ (II Cor. 3:18. Matt. 17:1-8).

THE CONSTRUCTION AND DEDICATION OF THE TABERNACLE. [Chs. 35 to 40.]

The Sabbath. (Ch. 35:1-3). These chapters are almost a verbal repetition of Chapters 25 to 31, as they describe the exact obedience to the Instructions given for the Construction of the Tabernacle. The content of these chapters may be summarized in these words: "According to all that the Lord commanded Moses, so the children of Israel made all the work" (Ch. 39:42).

However, as the instructions (Chs. 25-31) had closed with a solemn reference to the observance of the Sabbath (Ch. 31:12-17), so the record of the construction of the Tabernacle and its furniture is prefaced by a similar command to observe the seventh day as "an holy day, a Sabbath of rest unto the Lord." Thus every provision for a place of worship reminds the people of God that there are appointed times for worship and most specifically are they to "remember the sabbath day to keep it holy" (Ch. 35:1-3).

The Materials. (Chs. 35:4-36:7). The *materials* for the Tabernacle, exactly as described (Ch. 25:1-7), were provided by the free-will offerings of the people who were also invited to take part in the work of preparation. The great majority responded to the utmost of their power. It is implied that there were some whose hearts were not so stirred to sacrifice and to serve. However, enough and to spare was contributed until "the people were restrained from bringing, for the stuff they had was sufficient for all the work to make it, and too much" (Ch. 36:7).

The Preparation Completed. (Chs. 36:8-39:43). Bezaleel and Aholiab and their assistants undertook the work, and the parts of the Tabernacle were prepared as required in the instructions recorded in Chapter 26. The *curtains* (Ch. 26:31-36) were wrought of "fine linen, and blue and purple and scarlet," and the *coverings* (Ch. 26:1-14) of goats' hair, and rams' skins dyed red, and badger skins; and the *boards* of shittim wood were made ready and overlaid with gold (Ch. 26:15-30); and the beautiful *veil* was wrought with its ornaments of cherubim (Ch. 26:31-36), and the veil for the "door" of the holy place (Ch. 36:8-38).

The *ark* was constructed, and the mercy seat and the "*table of shewbread*" (Ch. 25:23-30), with its crown of gold and its rings and staves and vessels of gold; and the *candlestick* of gold (Ch. 25:31-40), with its branches and its lamps for the sacred oil; and the *altar of incense* (Ch. 30:1-10), with its obvious message of worship and adoration, the very climax of all the purpose of the Tabernacle (Ch. 37:1-29).

The *altar of burnt offering* (27:1-8) was constructed and overlaid with brass (38:1-7), and the *laver* (Ch. 30:17-21), here definitely described as made of "the looking glasses (polished mirrors of bronze) of women assembling, which assembled at the door of the tabernacle of the congregation" (38:8).

For the *court* which *surrounded the Tabernacle* (Ch. 27:9-19) the pillars are prepared, and the brazen sockets and the fillets and hooks of silver and the beautiful white curtains of fine twined linen (38:9-20).

An estimate is given as to the *value* of the *gold* and *silver* used in preparing for the sacred structure. It may be difficult to give the estimates in present-day measures, but the value of the gold may have been a million dollars, and of the silver more than two hundred thousand (Ch. 38:21-31).

The priestly *garments* were prepared with all the

richness described (Ch. 28:1-43), the ephod, the breast-plate, the robe, and the mitre. "According to all that the Lord commanded Moses, so the children of Israel did the work" (Ch. 39:1-43).

When all the preparation was completed, the Lord commanded Moses to wait until the first day of the first month before erecting the structure.

The Tabernacle Erected and Dedicated. (Ch. 40:1-38). Then on the day when it was reared up, a cloud covered the tent of the congregation and the glory of the Lord filled the Tabernacle. This cloud became the chariot of the King. When it moved, the Tabernacle and the camp of Israel moved, through all the journeying of the people. The coming of the cloud and the glory of the Lord filling the Holy of Holies were the symbolic dedication of the sacred shrine.

Thus the splendor of the Tabernacle lay not in its fine line, its blue and purple and scarlet, its silver and its gold, but in the manifested presence of Jehovah. Its ritual brought to the Israelites messages of divine holiness and mercy, of expiation and pardon, of access to God, and the conditions of worship and communion.

Its types and symbols found their fulfillment in the person and work of the Redeemer who "*dwelt* ["tabernacled"] among us full of grace and truth" (John 1:14). Its sacred image was in the mind of the seer when he "heard a great voice out of the throne saying, Behold the tabernacle of God is with men, and he will dwell with them, and they shall be his people, and God himself shall be with them and be their God" (Rev. 21:3).